To Barbara

In appreciation
for your response at the slide
show and in thanks for your
promo!

Lin

I Never Told
Anybody

Books by Kenneth Koch

Poems

Ko, or A Season on Earth

Permanently

Thank You and Other Poems

Bertha and Other Plays

When the Sun Tries to Go On

The Pleasures of Peace

Wishes, Lies, and Dreams:
Teaching Children to Write Poetry

A Change of Hearts:
Plays, Films, and Other Dramatic Works

Rose, Where Did You Get That Red?
Teaching Great Poetry to Children

The Art of Love

The Duplications

I Never Told Anybody:
Teaching Poetry Writing in a Nursing Home

I Never Told Anybody

TEACHING POETRY WRITING IN A
NURSING HOME

Kenneth Koch

Vintage Books

A Division of Random House
New York

First Vintage Books Edition, April 1978
Copyright © 1977 by Kenneth Koch

Grateful acknowledgment is made to the following for permission to reprint previously published material:

Alfred A. Knopf, Inc.: "Autobiographia Litteraria" by Frank O'Hara. Reprinted from *The Collected Poems of Frank O'Hara.* Copyright © 1967 by Maureen Granville-Smith, Administratrix of the Estate of Frank O'Hara. William Morrow & Co., Inc.: Four lines from the poem "The War God's Horse Song." Reprinted from *Magic World: American Indian Songs and Poems,* edited by William Brandon (1972).

New Directions Publishing Corp.: "Haiku" by Ryota. Reprinted from *One Hundred Poems From the Japanese,* edited by Kenneth Rexroth. All Rights Reserved. Reprinted by permission. Also, four lines of "The Last Words of My English Grandmother" and the poem "Nantucket" by William Carlos Williams. Reprinted from *Collected Earlier Poems* by William Carlos Williams. Copyright 1938 by New Directions Publishing Corporation.

Royal Anthropological Institute of Great Britain and Ireland: Seven lines from the African tribal poem "The Magnificent Bull," originally published in the 1904 issue of the *Journal of the Anthropological Institute.*

The Viking Press, Inc.: "The White Horse" by D. H. Lawrence. Reprinted from *The Complete Poems of D. H. Lawrence,* edited by Vivian de Sola Pinto and F. Warren Roberts. Copyright © 1964, 1971 by Angelo Ravagli and C. M. Weekley, Executors of the Estate of Frieda Lawrence Ravagli.

Library of Congress Cataloging in Publication Data

Koch, Kenneth, 1925-
    I never told anybody.

    1. Poetry—Study and teaching. 2. Aged, Writings
of the American. I. Title.
[PN1101.K55   1978]   808.1'0715   77-12704
ISBN 0-394-72499-2

Manufactured in the United States of America

To the Poets in the Workshop

Acknowledgments

Without Kate Farrell I don't believe I could have done this work; I know I couldn't have done it so well, or found out so much. Her teaching is a large part of what this book is about. She also helped me enormously in writing it. I am much indebted, too, to the American Nursing Home, and especially to Suzanne Uriel and Barbara Mittelmark. And to Poets and Writers and Hospital Audiences, who sponsored and helped organize the workshop; and to the volunteers from Hospital Audiences who helped in the teaching. To Margot Honig, Franklin Zawacki, and the Rhode Island Arts Council, which sponsored my first visit as a poetry teacher to an old-age home. To Jason and Barbara Epstein, who encouraged me to write this book. To Arlene Ladden and Ron Padgett, who visited the workshop and worked with me there and gave me their ideas. To David Lehman, who worked with me in several classes, then carried on the workshop after I left. And most of all, of course, to our students at the American Nursing Home, who wrote the poems.

Contents

Teaching Poetry Writing in a Nursing Home | 1
The Students' Poems | 59
Poems from Other Workshops | 229
The Poets | 256

Teaching Poetry Writing in a Nursing Home

AUTUMN

Your leaves were yellow
And some of them were darker
And I picked them up
And carried them in the house
And put them in different vases

Your leaves sound different
I couldn't understand why
The leaves at that time of year
Had a rustle about them
And they would drop
At the least little thing
And I would listen
And pick up some of them.

Nadya Catalfano

1

LAST spring and summer I taught poetry writing at the American Nursing Home in New York City. The American Nursing Home is on the Lower East Side, at Avenue B and Fifth Street. I had about twenty-five students, and we met sixteen times, usually on Wednesday mornings for about an hour. The students were all incapacitated in some way, by illness or old age. Most were in their seventies, eighties, and nineties. Most were from the working class and had a limited education. They had worked as dry cleaners, messengers, short-order cooks, domestic servants. A few had worked in offices, and one had been an actress. The nursing home gave them safety and care and a few activities, and sometimes a trip to a show or a museum. They did little or no reading or writing. They didn't write poetry.

I was assisted throughout by poet Kate Farrell, who, along with taking down students' poems and talking to them about their work, also helped me plan the lessons, and directed the workshop when I wasn't there. We always had the assistance, too, of one of the social workers (their official title is recreation director). Suzanne Uriel, the first with whom we worked, stopped regular work at the nursing home but kept coming back for most of the poetry classes. Barbara Mittelmark, who replaced Suzanne, was there from about the fifth session on. We were also assisted, for about ten classes, by two volunteers from Hospital Audiences, a group which, along with Poets and Writers, had helped me to find the American Nursing Home and to be able to teach there.

The idea to teach old and ill people to write poetry had come to me as a result of an interesting hour I spent working with poetry at the Jewish Old Age Home, in Providence, Rhode Island, and as a result of other hours, much less happy ones, I had spent as a visitor in nursing homes where nothing of that kind was going on. I wanted to see what could be done. I saw, even in their very difficult circumstances, possibilities for poetry—in the lives old people looked back on, in the time they had now to do that, and to think, and with a detachment hardly possible to them before. If, in the blankness and emptiness of a nursing home, they could write poetry, it would be a good thing—a

serious thing for them to work at, something worth doing
well and that engaged their abilities and their thoughts
and feelings.

I sensed this possibility, but it was evident that the
students I had at the American Nursing Home were re-
moved from poetry and from the writing of poetry in
many ways. None had written it before and none, I think,
would have begun without the workshop. The workshop
had to provide a bridge between what poetry was and what
the people there were—old, ill, relatively uneducated,
separated from their early lives, cautious about trying
anything new, afraid people might think them "finished,"
worthless, unable to do things well. They also had a conception of poetry likely to make it impossible for them to
write it well: the rhyming, metrical treatment of a certain
"poetical" subject matter. Not only were they unfamiliar
with poetry; they were quite out of the habit of learning,
of sitting in a room and hearing something explained.
These were problems aside from the physical ones. Some
had recent memory loss, were forgetful, tended to ramble
a little when they spoke. Everyone was ill, some people
sometimes in pain. Depression was frequent. A few were
blind, and some had serious problems in hearing. Several
students had severe speech problems and were very difficult, at first, to understand. To be added to all this was
their confinement within the walls and within the institu-
tional regime of the nursing home; they had little chance
to find, as poets usually do, fresh inspiration in new experiences, sights, and sounds. They lived without either
the city or nature to inspire their feelings. Poetry, if they
did write it, would have to come from memory and from
what happened and from what we could help make happen

right there in the nursing home. And almost none of our students were able to use their hands to write—either because of muscular difficulties or blindness.

Still, it is such a pleasure to say things, and such a special kind of pleasure to say them as poetry. I didn't, when I began, think much about the problems. I started, instead, with my feeling for the pleasure people could find in writing poetry, and assumed I could deal with any problems as they came up. My students, in fact, once given the chance to begin, were, in spite of all the difficulties, happy to be writing poems.

The method of teaching worked itself out as we went along. I began cautiously, asking people to think of a sentence or two. Then I suggested simple forms: Say three or four things about colors, and put the name of a color in every line. Gradually, encouraged by the students' success, I proposed bolder and bolder ideas: Imagine you are the ocean, and write a poem with every line beginning "I, the Ocean." Listen to this Keats sonnet and write a poem about talking to the moon or stars. In every class I suggested a kind of poem they should write. This gave ideas and relieved these hesitant, inexperienced students of the burden of finding a proper subject of their own. I said, "Write a poem about the quietest things or the quietest times you can think of; if you like, put a different quiet thing in every line."

The students told us their poems aloud, and we wrote them down. I was afraid this might not give them as much a sense of composing a work as writing would, but we found ways to do it that did: we were always reading lines back, saying "Here is what you've written so far," and "What do you want to say next?" The students' hesitancy and fear were much alleviated by our encouragement and admiration. My reading the poems aloud at the end of each class was an important part of this. It helped them to see that what they wrote was poetry and could be talked about seriously and admired. The teaching was based on the assumption that there is no insurmountable barrier between ordinary speech and poetry, and its aim was to help students move, easily and with confidence, from one to the other. Between the writer and the poem were no difficult demands of rhyme, metre, rhetoric, diction, or subject matter.

The kind of poetry I had in mind as a model was the unrhymed, nonmetrical, fairly unliterary poetry of such poets as D. H. Lawrence, Walt Whitman, and William Carlos Williams, poetry with music and language like this—

> The youth goes up to the white horse to put its
>   halter on
> And the horse looks at him in silence.
> They are so silent they are in another world.
>
> > D. H. Lawrence, "The White Horse"

or like this—

> I think I will do nothing for a long time but listen
> And accrue what I hear into myself . . . and let
>   sounds contribute toward me.
> I hear the bravuras of birds . . . the bustle of growing
>   wheat . . .
>
> > Walt Whitman, "Song of Myself"

or this—

> There were some dirty plates
> and a glass of milk
> beside her on a small table
> near the rank, dissheveled bed . . .

> W. C. Williams, "The Last Words
> of My English Grandmother"

Such poetry, with its combination of prosiness, talky quality, repetition, and lyricism, if not something many writers can completely master, is also not completely unapproachable. A modestly educated, unliterary old person can have a chance of writing something like it. He can use the natural strengths for poetry he has: the music of ordinary speech and the memories and feelings his long life has given him. Asked to rhyme or to use metre or any difficult forms, or to write about mythology or metaphysics, I think most of our students would have written nothing at all.

Our students didn't know there was a poetry like that I read to them. Hearing it encouraged them to write and made my praise of their work more intelligible, too. Having read them D. H. Lawrence's "The White Horse," I could say how, in Fred Richardson's poem, the repetition of *quiet*, like Lawrence's near repetition of *silence* and *silent*, gives a sensation of conclusion and finality, and how coming down on the same word *quiet* makes a very quiet sound—

> I always was quiet
> And my mother always had to send my
> sisters into the room
> To see what made me so quiet.

Our students didn't know, very consciously at any rate, that repetition, for example, was a part of poetry, or comparisons, or personification, or exaggeration. They didn't know that details were good to have in a poem—details of color, of weather, of sound. They didn't know what kind of language could be in a poem, or what kind of form. I taught them what poetry could be, by suggesting subjects and forms, by reading them great poems, and by reading aloud and commenting on their work. It was starting from the beginning in every way, but it didn't take them long to get a sense of what poetry is. Such a sense seems, and how could it not be, a fairly natural one for people to have. They had it once poetry was no longer something forbidding and remote but something near, familiar, and beautiful; as near as their feelings about a color—

> I like green; I used to see so many greens on
> the farm.
> I used to wear green, and sometimes my mother
> couldn't find me
> Because I was green in the green.

Mary Tkalec

or as their memories of a quiet time—

> The quietest night I remember
> Was going out deep-sea fishing.
> Me and my friend were way out on a rowboat
>   fishing.
> We caught a lot of fish.
> All the stars were shining
> The ocean was quiet
> The wind was quiet
> And we were quiet
> And the fish were biting.
>
> Leroy Burton

These two poems were written for the second and third classes. Both are pretty good examples of how quickly the students could move from ordinary conversational prose to poetry, with the help of a suggested (and arbitrary) theme and a suggested (repetitive) form, and with an approachable poetic model to emulate. Some of Leroy Burton's lines are very different from the prose in which he spoke—

> ... The ocean was quiet
> The wind was quiet
> And we were quiet
> And the fish were biting.

The "poetry ideas," the suggestions for form and content I gave each time, were important for providing subjects (good, evocative ones), for directing the students' speech toward the slight arbitrariness of poetry (put a color in every line), and for teaching new things about poetry (comparisons, for example, or personification). They also helped provide the excitement and surprise that are part of poetic inspiration, and which were lacking in nursing-home life. The ideas were usually accompanied by other things. For poems about music, we brought in and played records of Vivaldi and of New Orleans jazz. For other poems we brought in flowers or sea shells, seaweed, driftwood, and sand. Whenever possible, I read other poems aloud. For the quietness class, for example, I read not only "The White Horse" but also Williams' "Nantucket" and a haiku, by the Japanese poet Ryota, about a very silent evening—

No one spoke
The host, the guests,
The white chrysanthemums.

To make the strangeness and the quietness of that perhaps closer to my students, I invented a similar poem about the workshop room—

No one spoke,
Kate, Suzanne,
The white chairs.

When I asked them to write to the moon or stars I read Keats's sonnet "Bright star! Would I were steadfast as thou art." For poems on Being the Ocean I read passages on the ocean from Whitman ("And you, Sea, I think I know what you want . . .") and Byron ("Roll on, thou deep and dark blue ocean, roll! . . .")

Poetry, which seemed so distant from the students when we began, became natural to them. At first, unfamiliar with it, reluctant to write it, some unwilling to talk at all, they soon found it possible to write about almost anything and found nothing strange in our bringing in seaweed, Christmas lights, or Chinese poems, for example, to give them inspiration. Poetry gave them a new reason for looking at things and for remembering them: to say what they thought and felt.

2

The workshop was in a large room on the fourth floor of the nursing home. It adjoined the TV room, which caused the minor distractions of noise and people going back and forth. When Kate and I arrived, the students were still arriving (there were about twenty-five of them), most being wheeled in in wheelchairs, some with walkers, only a few able to walk without assistance. In chairs or wheelchairs, they were finally all seated at two long tables perpendicular to the small table I stood at to talk to them. Kate and our assistants sat on the side. I did all the talking at the start. When we took down students' lines, each of us would go and sit down with one at a time.

The students, whom I was soon to know as individuals, seemed this first time very much alike. They seemed old, sick, tired, uncomfortable. Some seemed to be asleep or almost so. Others stared around distractedly. One or two showed signs of being in pain. Some looked at me in a pleasant and friendly, if slightly puzzled, way. Suzanne had chosen people for the workshop mainly on the basis of their articulateness and sociability. These standards didn't include a knowledge of poetry or of what was going to happen in the workshop. Suzanne introduced me and said we were going to do poetry. I introduced Kate and the volunteers from Hospital Audiences, then said a few more things about myself—that I was a poet and a professor at Columbia.

What I was going to do, I said, was to have them write poetry. I said how much I liked to write it myself and also that it need not be the difficult and painful thing that many people think. I had a kind of poetry in mind and a way of writing it that I thought they would like. The nursing-home residents were nodding yes, but of course were just as puzzled as ever until they had actually begun to do something. As I looked out over the room, I did wonder then, for the last time, if what I was proposing to do was really possible. If we hadn't started to write, both their doubts and mine could have gone on forever. In the first class my main purpose was simply to get the students to write (or say) something. Each student would write a sentence. Once I had sentences from all, my plan was to read them back together as one poem. The speed, ease, and surprisingness of this procedure would, I believed, excite the students and make them want to write more.

I proposed a collaborative poem about childhood memories. What I actually said was that I wanted everyone to think of some small thing he remembered from his childhood. I said, "Think of the place you were born. And think of something you remember about that place. Something about the house you had as a child, maybe. The color of the bedroom walls. The kinds of flowers that grew outside. Or the clothes you wore. Or a pet you had. Make it something really small, and talk about things like colors and sounds and the way things feel. Use the name of the town or country you were born in. And if it fits, use the actual names of people or animals or streets. When everyone has written a memory like that, I'll put them together and we'll have a poem. Then I'll read it aloud. Everybody will write one thing. It can be about absolutely anything, so long as it's about the place you were born—and make it something particular, with colors, if possible, and names."

If this sounds repetitive, it's because it was. I couldn't be sure that people were catching on to what I said. Some students had difficulty hearing, and most were so unaccustomed to listening the way what I was saying demanded (they weren't used to courses or lectures) that that too might have made me hard to understand. I went on to asking them questions. Suzanne had told me they were born in a variety of places. People are usually slightly fascinated by the fact of having been born someplace, and the questions about birthplace got a good response. There were students born in Scotland, Sweden, Barbados, Austria, and Poland, as well as in different parts of the United States. I asked them to tell me some things they remembered about those places. Responses were sometimes just silence; or "I was born there, that's all"; "It's a wonderful country." Some were more specific: "I remember we had a lot of dogs on the farm." My questions, to this last, were "What were their names? What color were they? Which one did you like best?" My questions to the silence or to vague responses were "What was your house like? What was your favorite thing to do when you were a child?" I kept asking for smaller and more precise details, just those that most seemed reluctant to give, perhaps because they thought them unimportant and silly. How did they know they wouldn't be thought foolish if they talked about playing with their dog or what color their babyhood pajamas were? People usually think best of themselves for making general statements, and those also seem the safest. I gave examples from my own life: the blue bike my father gave me when I was five, on which I rode up and down Mitchell Avenue; the Cincinnati Reds baseball games I went to with my grandfather, and my fear of asking the soft-drink man to give me something. I said one remembers strange things, or rather it's strange what one remembers, not always things one thought would be most important. I encouraged them to just say the first thing that came to mind.

All this, in a shorter version, we did again when we took down the lines. Person-to-person confirmation of what I'd said made it clearer and more appealing. A few students couldn't, or wouldn't, tell us anything, but most did. Much of the collaborative poem was fairly general and prosy, but there were enough remembered, specific things to make it pleasant to hear. That is what we wanted, an attractive text to read back to the students which would make them feel good about writing and want to write more. There were lines likeable for their feeling, for their humor, or simply for the information they gave—

> I remember the national colors of Sweden—
> yellow and blue. . . .
> The ocean in the Barbados was very nice—
> a big wide sea. . . .

> I did so much devilment until I didn't know my
> own self. I went to bed with my dog. . . .

I shuffled the pages and read the lines off as a poem. I
read the lines with pleasure and admired a lot of things,
sometimes stopping to comment on just what I thought
was so good about them. People were excited at the unaccustomed pleasure of hearing what they said read aloud,
and excited at hearing it admired by me and by other
students. For the students were quite responsive to the
poem, commenting on the beauty of something said or on
its truth to their experience, as Mary L. Jackson did on
hearing William Ross's memories of his first pair of long
pants—

> . . . They couldn't tell me anything when I had
> that pair of pants. . . .

"Oh, I know, I know," Mary L. Jackson said, smiling and
looking around to see who might have written that (I
didn't give the names this time of writers of particular
lines).

My comments on what they wrote were, as always, positive. I looked, in the fundamentally prosy work they gave
me, for whatever had any quality that I liked in poetry
and that would be good for them to be aware of and think
of using later. This included sensuous detail, humor, talking about strong feelings, some energetic personal way of
saying something. There was humor in the line about

going to bed with the dog, in the story of the long pants, and in that of Minnie the Cat—

> Once we had measles, the cat thought we needed
> extra nourishment and brought us more.

Humor is good to point out and praise. Like many kinds of poetic statement, it is a spirited form of language. What is said and how it is said makes one laugh, causes a physical reaction as metaphor does, and it is a departure from ordinary fact-recounting prose. There was little about sense impressions in this poem. I admired anything that suggested them, such as the naming of Sweden's national colors: yellow and blue; saying of the ocean in Barbados that it was "a big wide sea." I admired the truth and the dreaminess of these recollections of a street—

> . . . I always wondered about the name of the street,
> Amber Street. I always thought there must
> be something to the name Amber. . . .

I said that I had wondered about things like that, too, and that when I lived in France, in Paris, on the rue du Cherche Midi, I always wondered about that name but never found out where it came from. It could mean the street of Searching for the South, or the street of Searching for Noon. Nice names for a street, and quite mysterious. One student wrote about her sadness over a cat that died—

> . . . When someone killed it, I cried like a baby.
> My mother said, "What? Are you crying
> like that over a cat?" But dumb beasts
> like that, you get to love them. . . .

I admired this little story of sadness and incomprehension
and said so. I liked the student's talking about something
strong and emotional that might seem silly to others.
Mostly the collaborative poem had the sound of prose. I
stopped to admire anything in it that had a suggestion of
music—such as this about the sea:

> I used to go in every blessèd day as a girl. . . .

or

> . . . I thought I was a big deal in that long pair of
> pants. I thought I was as big as my father in
> those pants. . . .

I said how good those things sounded.

My commenting and praising this first time was, essen-
tially, finding poetic elements in a prose text, so as to give
its authors confidence and courage to do more, and better.
There was nothing false about it. I did in fact admire the
qualities in the poem that I praised. In the work of more
sophisticated poets I would pass over most of those things,
because others would preempt my attention. But at the
beginning, when someone is learning to dance, say, one
admires what grace and balance and control there are,
and they are really admirable. The professional dancer
makes a beautiful work of them, as a painter may make a

beautiful painting out of red, green, yellow, and white. But those colors are bright, beautiful, and even moving in themselves. And so were these materials of poetry in my students' first text. I praised them to show that they were there and to give those who'd written them ideas for using them again.

I gave them a chance to use them again immediately, for, since there were fifteen or twenty minutes left, and since the class was in an excited mood, I proposed they do another collaboration right away. This time the theme I suggested was beauty. "Think of the most beautiful thing you have ever seen, absolutely the most beautiful. When were you really moved and excited by how beautiful something was? It can be a landscape, a mountain, the ocean, anything you saw in nature. Or a person. Who was the most beautiful person you ever saw? It could be a dress, a painting, a building, anything. You might try closing your eyes and thinking hard about it, the most beautiful thing you ever saw." As before, I gave examples, asked for some responses from them. I was a little more hurried, though. There wasn't much time, and the main thing I wanted was for them to write again, there in that same class, in that same mood of excitement about experiences and words. This second poem did in fact turn out to be more sensuous, more detailed, and more surprising than the first. The subject, beauty, which is probably more stirring than merely any childhood memory, had something to do with it, but there was also the mood and what they had just learned from what they'd written and what I had said. Again I urged them to be particular and to think of how things really looked. I mentioned, among other examples, the white angora sweater of a girl I took out in high school. I thought it was the most beautiful thing I'd ever seen.

As with the first poem, we explained the idea again, when necessary, to individual students. Not so many needed it this time. Reading the poem aloud, I again praised things precisely seen and felt—

> Redwood trees I saw in California—their
> tallness and their huge trunks. . . .

> . . . beautiful girls with bikinis on, on Jones
> Beach. . . .

and the humor, which this time seemed more thoughtful and surprising—

> The most beautiful thing I ever saw was my first
> dollar bill—so I could buy candy for my
> childhood sweetheart. . . .

as well, this time, as the judgment reflected in the choices they made—

> The locks at Sault Sainte Marie, making air where
> the ships go through. . . .

In this class, one could see in little what happened throughout the workshop: suggestions leading to works, works to admiration, excitement, and thought, and those to new suggestions and new works.

For each of these collaborative poems I had the students choose a title. Poems almost always do have titles, and having one made theirs more the real thing. I never regarded anything they did as "practice," to be followed by "And soon we'll be ready to write a poem." I preferred having them write one at once and give it the kind of attention a poem gets. I didn't treat anything in the class as merely preparation for something more authentic to come. Students thrive most on achievement. Choosing a title not only made the class collaborations more like other poems but also gave the students a chance to think about the whole poem, with all its diverse contributions, at once, and have more of a sense of what it was like.

I proposed they make suggestions for a title, and then vote on the one they liked best. This caused pleasant reflection this first time, if not too many suggestions. The winning title was rather tame, but everyone seemed pleased with it: "American Nursing Home Poem." It was natural enough to call it that when it was the only one. For the second collaboration, the title was "Beautiful."

It was a good first class. The students had been willing to write. They had been excited at hearing what they wrote. And they had been willing to write a second poem. In one hour, in difficult circumstances, they had done something new and even progressed at it, for the second poem seemed even better than the first.

Class collaborations were a good beginning. They take pressure off individuals and encourage brief and spontaneous contributions. Collaborating also creates a slightly festive atmosphere, being in some respects like a party game—everyone contributing his sentences, then hearing the surprising results. One can laugh at them or feel unexpected admiration. In the writing of individual poems, which the students began to do next, we were able to keep much of this feeling of excitement and ease. Though people wrote more lines, again everyone wrote on the same subject, and everyone heard the results a little later, read aloud, together—not as one poem this time, but still read all at once, and with admiration.

3

The poetry idea in the second class, for their first individual poems, was Color. "Think of your favorite color or a color you like a lot, and write about what it makes you think of. Put the name of the color, if you like, in every line or so." Colors had been one thing I liked in the first collaborations, and I wanted to encourage their use. The next poetry idea was Quiet Things and Quiet Times. Instead of sense associations, this time the students concentrated on moods. Next was a Lie Poem, to show the possibilities in departing from ordinary prose reality, of bringing in the purely imaginary. For the next class we brought in flowers. For the first time, poems could be about present perceptions as well as about the past. Next were poems written while listening to music. Childhood memories, beautiful things, colors, and quiet times were, in our class, good ideas to start with. But there was nothing inevitable about them or about their order. More important was that the idea be different every time and give the students, as much as possible, something to do in poetry they hadn't yet done.

The class on writing poetry to music was so good that I gave another one, but two were enough. It was good to go on from "hearing" feelings in music to touching things (lace, velvet, lemons, ribbon, Christmas ornament, sea shell) and "feeling" memories and emotions in those—

Lace,
It makes me think of a tent
Out in the open where children play . . .

Peggy Marriott

and to go from there to being able to touch, smell, and look at a collection of sea shells, seaweed, sand, and stones and write a poem imagining they had all these things beneath them, beside or inside them, that they were the sea—a new way of dealing with feelings and perceptions: personification, being someone or something else—

. . . Everyone is afraid of my temper
But I soon cool off
And everyone is happy again
My company is all happy again
All the fish are glad, especially the small ones
Because they are the most helpless during the
    storms.

Rose MacMillan

and, later, after writing poetry had become a part of their experience, to have them write about that, which was the first time they wrote about their associations with something they themselves were doing—

I like the idea of poetry
It gives me a chance to explain my life and
    my childhood days
Because ever since I was five or six years old
    I was a very busy kid . . .

                        Leroy Burton

Poetry is like being in Inner Space . . .

                        William Ross

If I repeated an idea in one way, I tried to make it different in another. We used flowers again in the last class, but this time asked the students to write collaborative poems as they looked at them, and then to take the parts of different flowers in a poetic play.

Some things about the poetry ideas remained the same. They were always about feelings, impressions, and associations. They always asked for personal responses. They invited thinking of and remembering small things, particular details, especially those connected with feeling and sensation. They approached strong emotions in indirect ways, asking, for example, not for poems about childhood longings or about feelings for nature, but for a poem of talking to the moon or the stars. In the course of writing such a poem, these feelings, hard to get to directly, might be come on by surprise—

Oh moon and stars
I loved to watch you
When I was a child

I would watch you through my little window
And wonder and worry
What would happen if you got hurt
And next time I'd say
"Oh, you're still living!". . .

Mary Tkalec

Asking directly for writing about love, life, time, child-hood, and so on tends to make people's minds go blank as they search for conventional and general statements which will be the "right answer." One needn't be afraid such feelings won't come up, since so many memories and de-tails of life are connected to them. Our students wrote about love, for example, when the poetry ideas were talk-ing to the moon, poetry, comparisons, touch, writing while listening to music, and I never told anybody—

I write poems about going to school
And about home and about the old friends
About love and being together with Al
I don't know whether he likes me or not . . .

Laura Bradshaw

I never told anybody that I drove away in a
buggy . . .

Mary L. Jackson

This powder puff makes me think of your hair . . .

Sam Rainey

The one time I did ask directly for feelings about a "big and important subject"—a poem on feelings about growing older—students for the most part got stuck in conventional feelings and generalizations. Even in its small details I wanted the poetry idea not to be phrased in such a way as to invite inhibition and, with it, conventionality. A poem about quiet things and quiet times was a better suggestion than a poem about "peaceful times." The word *peaceful*, I think, suggests attitudes, whereas *quiet* suggests feelings.

Another constant feature of the poetry ideas was proposing a certain form—always some kind of repetition or listing. This seemed a formal organizing principle for poems which was not too far from my students' natural speech, which would not be too difficult for them to learn, and which would give what they wrote some of the disconnectedness and surprising juxtapositions of poetry, as well as providing it with a structure. I sometimes asked them to repeat a word (Put the name of the color in every line or so) or a phrase (Start every line or so with the words "I never told anybody"—or "I, the Ocean"). Sometimes I asked for repetition, or listing, of a certain kind of content (in every line or so put a different thing the music reminds you of) or of a rhetorical device (in every line or two make a different comparison). The formal element made their poems clearly different from what they usually said, thus making poetry something distinct. It organized memories and feelings in a way that, by putting them in a new order, showed new things about them, and which could cause the writer, coming on them this way by surprise, to be moved by them and to communicate that emotion in what was said—

All I know is the white sheep
And that I used to watch the collie
Taking the sheep home.
I remember my Communion in my white veil,
And my Confirmation, and my marriage. . . .

                    Rose MacMillan

The repetitive form also helped students get a sense of
writing in lines. In addition to the natural syntactic pause,
the presence of some repeated element could determine the
unity of a line—

I can remember a dress trimmed in silver
And silver slippers . . .

                    Helen Lesser

With repetition and listing the students could get more
of poetry's content and form without losing anything good
that was naturally theirs, in language or in what they had
to say. They could help in the transition, say, from the
loose conversational charm of this recollection—

Our cat's name was Minnie. She used to catch
    birds and little rabbits. Our grandmother
    used to clean them and make them into soup. . . .

            Mary L. Jackson, 1st class

to the more musical and formal charm of this one—

> Riding on the freight trains
> And the boxcars
> And singing
> They were so happy
> That they were coming home.
>
> Mary L. Jackson, 13th class

or of this—

> I once had a secret love but I never told anybody
> I once ran away but I never told anybody
> Once when I was walking down the street
> I saw a man running with a gun in his hand
> But I never told anybody . . .
>
> Mary L. Jackson, 15th class

Rhyme is another formal element one might consider, but it would not have helped our students make this kind of transition. Unfortunately, for inexperienced writers, rhyme tends to destroy or at best to dull the qualities one hopes that form will help create. When our students used it, their work was quite inferior to what they otherwise wrote—like this first stanza of "Memories" by William Ross—

Memories are made of things
That happen every day
The moments as we live them
Things we do or say . . .

which may be compared to a characteristic product of
William's talent, written two months earlier—

Roses are the stand-out flower among flowers.
They're just like a beautiful woman—
Can't help from being noticed,
Especially American Beauties.

Rhyme and metre aren't unteachable or never to be
taught, but in the short time we were at the nursing home
they were not something students were able to have without losing too much of what they had gained. Had I stayed,
I would have encouraged William to try ways of using
rhyme without his poetry's losing the good qualities it
already had. But as an alchemy to change prose to poetry,
repetition was, for my students, much, much better.

A certain daring in the poetry ideas always turned out
to be good. Nothing I did was any bolder than what I had
done at the start, in asking them to write poetry. Some of
my most successful ideas I was hesitant about: listening to
music, being the ocean, talking to the moon. The music
I thought might be too loud and gay for the nursing home.
Being the ocean seemed a little outrageous—to ask these
people to identify themselves with the powerful sea. Talk-

ing to moon or stars, and using Keats's sonnet to inspire it, seemed inappropriately youthful and romantic. There are several reasons for the kind of doubts I had. One is a hush-hushy feeling about old people, the feeling that what they really want and need is quiet and peace; the other is that these subjects, all having to do with power, energy, and passion, will cause them pain and make them feel empty, because they will feel unconnected to them, being, themselves, weak and infirm. Both ideas are wrong. Strong feelings don't vanish. Passion and energy are what life is all about, and most of the time people can identify with them easily, as I can with Hamlet on the stage or with Superman, or with an aria in *The Magic Flute*. What a teacher should do is not protect his students from experiencing strong feelings, but look for ways to help them to express such feelings. Physical disability didn't keep my students from responding enthusiastically to music—in this case, New Orleans jazz—

This makes my ribs move
I had an accident a couple days ago
I couldn't move
But my ribs are beginning to move
The doctor almost gave me up
Till I heard that music
Then I started to move

Mary Tkalec

nor did their inactive, indoors, physically restricted life interfere with their ability to identify themselves with the ocean, in its peaceful aspects as well as in its wildest and most destructive—

> . . . When I'm angry
> All hell breaks loose
> Again I can be so beautiful
> When I'm calm . . .
>
> William Ross

> . . . I can rock boats and wreck them
> Pounding and breaking . . .
>
> Mary Tkalec

My students found it easy to talk to moon and stars, as well as to be influenced by Keats's sonnet, for all its purely youthful passion and its unfamiliar language and references—

> Bright star! Would I were steadfast as thou art—
> Not in lone splendour hung aloft the night . . .

Here, it was just a question of my reading Keats's poem slowly twice, explaining words and ideas, and saying what I liked. William Ross had some of the feelings and tone of the Keats poem already in a poem he told Kate he had begun during the week and which he finished in this class—

LOVE SONG

Belovèd, I have to adore the earth:
The wind must have had your voice once.
It echoes and sings like you.
The soil must have tasted you once.
It is laden with your scent.
The trees honor you in gold and blush when you
    pass.
I know why the North Country is frozen.
It has been trying to preserve your memory.
I know why the desert burns with fever.
It wept too long without you.
On hands and knees the ocean begs up the beach
And falls at your feet.
I have to adore the mirror of the earth.
You have taught her well how to be beautiful.

4

After the poetry idea was presented, the students, in most cases, dictated their poems to us. Dictation, necessary because of physical disability, such as muscular and visual difficulties, was helpful to students whose limited education would have caused them worries about the correctness of their writing—spelling, grammar, and so on. Speaking their poems made it much easier, especially at the start, but I think, too, throughout the workshop. My students in general felt easier and more relaxed about talking than about writing, had command of more words and had more chance to say things musically, humorously, colorfully, and movingly. Dictating the poems also created a time for individual teaching, in which a great deal of the work of the course took place.

Working alone with them, we did more than take down poems: we encouraged students to begin, and, once begun, to stay on the subject, to think again of what they had written, to write more. We clarified the poetry idea, went on talking about it, gave examples, and intensified its effect on the students, the purpose being always the same: to make poetry writing easy and to teach by means of experience and inspiration. We helped students have confidence in themselves and in their ability to make up poems. We helped them to a feeling for the beauty of what they were saying. We read their lines back to them, saying, "That is what you have so far. It's good. I especially like such and such. What do you want to add now?" Only three or four students, I think, could have written at first without these small conferences. And, without them, even they would probably not have progressed so quickly.

At the beginning of the workshop our students were in different stages of readiness for writing poetry. Some seemed ready to write and learn almost at once. Other students were willing to talk to us and to have us transcribe it, but remained unsure for some time as to the distinction between regular talk and composing a poem. They might chat in a rambling sort of way about some subject, or tell us a story, or give us information. With these students it was important to stay with the poetry idea and always bring them back to it—by reading back whatever on the subject they had already written, by questions and suggestions (What about clothes? the color of a car? What is another thing about blue that you remember?). The students were good-natured about doing this odd thing—making associations with the color blue, for instance—

which demanded an unfamiliar kind of reflection. We kept reading back the results, asking if there were more, or did the poem end there?

For some students it was hard to begin to tell us things and let us take them down. They said, "I don't remember anything" or "I can't think." We would say, "Of course you can. Listen, tell me, where were you born?" "What town did you grow up in? What kind of house?" I told them that I had lived in a house with a huge basement, where I had my chemistry set. Almost always struck by some example or question, the student would tell us something, and we could ask if he wanted to begin the poem with something about that, and, if so, how he wanted to say it. When he told us a line, we would read it back to him and say, "All right, that's the first line. What do you want to say next?"

It was a happy time, for us and for the student, when someone overcame serious hesitations and began to like writing, as Nadya Catalfano did, in the sixth class, the one on writing while listening to music. At first refusing to say anything, Nadya did finally, at Kate's urging, tell her something—

> The only thing I can think of is my grandmother's
> going to give me a whipping if I do this or that—

Kate said, "That's fine. Shall we begin the poem with that?" Nadya's line was good in the way it went back into the past dramatically, as if what happened then were happening now. And her being transported that way promised good things to come if she would go on talking about that memory the music inspired. To Kate's question, Nadya at first said, No, she didn't want that written down. She said it was not poetry, was "not anything." Kate encouraged her to tell her more, which, in spite of her doubts, Nadya did. Then she was very unsure about the value of what she had said:

> The only thing I can think of is my grandmother's
> going to give me a whipping if I do this or
> that.
> There was a log house and steps.
> I was an only child
> And my mother was away working . . .

Kate said, "That's beautiful, that short line about the log house after the long first one. It really makes me see it, as if it had just suddenly gotten clear. What you wrote is very pretty. It's good poetry." Nadya said, "Oh, really? I thought it was childish." She meant that it wasn't serious because it was just what she remembered about being a silly little child. Kate assured her that such "childish" things were important in poetry. She read it back to her again. Nadya liked it. Even more, it seemed, when I read it aloud, and other people responded to it as well. After that, Nadya really liked writing poetry, and often talked to Kate about what it was like to be a poet. What happened was that Nadya found out that what she considered a silly weakness in herself, or at least a secret pleasure no one else would care about, her thinking all the time about "little things," was something she could do something with in poetry. She wrote, later,

There's a lot of little things that I think about.
I think about them to write them down . . .
Flowers I like to see them grow.
I like to see them blossom.
I go and pick them up and put them in books
And save them.
I love to smell them.
I think I hear them.
It seems to me they answer me back . . .

Once she had begun, Nadya wrote some fine, bold poems, such as this one, which she entitled "The Call," written in the class on Touch, which was just after the music class, about the feel of a thin gold necklace—

Something soft and gentle
Glides through your fingers
And it seems to grab your hand and lead you
On to something greater
If only you had the sense to follow it .

Sometimes a setback of some kind, a feeling of weakness, illness, or depression, would make it hard for a student to write. We thought that if he had come to the workshop that day, it was probably because he would like to be able to write, and we would talk to him about how he felt, and usually, after talking for a while, the student would write something and be glad to have done it. Sometimes, especially in the early classes, a student would grow discouraged, or be bothered by the effort of making up a poem and tell us, "You say it—you can say it better than I." We said, "You are the only one who can. It's your poem." Having strong feelings unexpectedly, as often happens in writing poetry, sometimes someone would feel overwhelmed and start to cry. That seemed natural enough—it's not unusual to cry when one is writing. We would wait, and talk about what caused the crying, and always, after talking about it, the student would want to go on with the poem, and would be glad on hearing it read aloud. Tears were something on the way to the poem and not anything that made the writer unhappy afterward. Most of the students, most of the time, were in good form for the class. When they were not, it was usually not hard to help them to be, especially once they had come to enjoy writing.

Especially at first, the dictation part could be very slow. Later, often, when the students knew more, and when the poetry idea stirred them, they wrote quickly and sometimes made up two or more poems in a class. I remember Nadya, the week after her conversion to poetry with Kate, writing two of them, one with Kate and one with me. In the music class, impressed by the students' enthusiasm, I asked everyone to write two poems. It was always a good idea, when there was time, and someone had written a poem, to ask him whether he wanted to do another. Sometimes writing one made a student excited and gave him ideas for the next. Sometimes writing more than one gave him a chance to revise or in some way change his original conception, as Nadya did, for example, in the two poems she wrote about the necklace.

Working with students in later classes, we could sometimes concentrate on some special problem, or opportunity, that we'd seen in their writing. Margaret Whittaker, for example, I thought witty and talented, but her poetry had not so far escaped from being rather prosy and dry. In the I Never Told Anybody class, I proposed she rewrite the poem she had already done and this time write it as if the events it described were happening right now—she did that, and in doing it wrote a good, dramatic poem—saying, for example, instead of "I wanted people to ask me to dance" (first version) —

> I'm sitting here and wondering
> How many are going to ask me to dance tonight . . .

It was good to have people to assist me in talking to students and taking down their poems. Not only because of how it helped with time (transcribing twenty-five poems could have taken more than an hour, maybe two hours, and what would those who weren't dictating be doing all that time?), but also because students were sometimes able to talk to Kate, or to Suzanne or Barbara in a way they might not have talked to me, and wrote things they might not have otherwise written. With Suzanne and Barbara, whom they knew, the students sometimes talked more freely about themselves. And Kate has a special talent for giving confidence and for helping people talk about their feelings. At the beginning, students tended to write somewhat differently for different transcribers—much less so later on. I could have carried on the workshop as we did with only one person to help me. Alone in a class of that size, I would have used many more class collaborations, of the kind I used in the Roses class, in which everyone is looking at or thinking about the same thing and everyone hears what everyone else has to say. That way, interest and excitement are kept up. And there would be time, too, for individual poems, for it often happens that students, stirred by a collaborative poem, have a poem of their own come to mind that they can dictate quickly.

In many groups, of course, all or most of the students will be able to write. Of if some are, and others are not able to, those who are can transcribe poems for the others.

5

Reading the poems aloud was important for the students' pleasure and continuing interest in poetry, and also for their learning more about it. It was best when it came just after the poems were written. I read them all, liking and commenting on things. One doesn't have to be an expert in poetry to make such comments, but just to be able to show that one likes something that is funny or beautiful or well said, that makes one remember something or want to laugh or cry. I responded sometimes to details, sometimes to a whole poem.

Some examples from the classes on writing to music will give a general idea of my comments. Other people might admire other things. It is important to show the admiration. The music suggested this brief poem to Carmela Pagluca—

The ocean—
The waves and the beach—
It reminds me of my childhood days

I found the poem touching and said so. I said I liked the idea of the music sounding like the ocean; the way the lines got longer, as if stronger, as a wave does when it comes to the shore; the feeling of sadness. Another poem (by William Ross) began like this:

This music reminds me of a multitude of colors . . .

I loved the word *multitude*; it was an abstract word that made you see something, and seemed to go very well with the sound of *colors*. The image that followed this first line was beautiful and rich. It made one see the colors and also something new—

Like petals from flowers floating through the air . . .

after this was another comparison—

Also like a ballet group dancing on the stage . . .

I said how much I liked the going from one comparison to another—the music like colors, like flower petals, like dancers. It made them all seem like the same thing in some magical way. The dancers had the lightness and grace of flower petals. The colors were moving like dancers. After talking about lines, I often read them aloud again, to give others a chance to see the good qualities I'd described. One student was reminded by the music of a fire—

> . . . I thought I could see flames in the music
> I thought I could see people running with a
>   lot of excitement . . .
>
>   Tom O'Neil

Here I admired the vision—that the music made the writer really see something so strongly and his poem made it clear he saw it strongly by giving such details—the people running made the fire seem more real. Mary L. Jackson was reminded, among other things, of being

> . . . At a dinner—something large—dancing and
>   eating pheasant
> Or riding through Central Park on a warm day.

I really liked the details and the very real and particular things the music made her think of. I liked the way the lines seemed to be trying to make something, like a dream or a vision, become clearer:

> At a dinner—something large—dancing . . .

I said that was a good way to describe something, as if one were just seeing it and didn't necessarily already know all about it—that's the way things really happen. I said her poem reminded me of Whitman, the kind of thing he talks about in his long lists of what is going on in America all at the same time—

The married and unmarried children ride
home to their thanksgiving dinner—

I liked the detail "on a warm day"—it made the ride in the
park seem real. It's so nice to hear about the weather. It's
good to put something about it in poems. I much admired
the humor of Mary Tkalec's lines about the music's having
a curative effect on her—

This makes my ribs move . . .
The doctor almost gave me up
Until I heard that music . . .

When Sam Rainey wrote

The music reminds me of a mountain

I said, "That's terrific. What a beautiful thing for music
to remind one of—a mountain." There was also the beautiful image that came later on—

. . . And it sounds like the wind blowing
Against the house
And the heavy rain blowing on the roof
And now and again with the lightning . . .

I especially liked how much the added details about the rain and the lightning made the scene and the comparison seem much more real, much more so than if he had merely written

> And it sounds like the wind blowing
> Against the house . . .

My comments never took very much time. I said what I liked and why, sometimes reread a line or two, then moved on to the next poem. Even if many students didn't understand all the points I made, they understood some, and heard me praising their poems, and heard me saying and repeating their lines. They heard their poems, composed, sometimes with difficulty, such a short time before, read aloud and admired. That consolidated, validated in a way, like some sort of instant publication, what they had accomplished.

6

Our students did accomplish things. I am not sure that helped them to adjust to life in the nursing home. Rather, I think, it slightly changed the conditions of that life, which was better. I don't think I would like to adjust to a life without imagination or accomplishment, and I don't believe my students wanted to either. It is in that sense, perhaps, that it can best be understood why it is better to teach poetry writing as an art than to teach it—

well, not really teach it but use it—as some form of distracting or consoling therapy. As therapy it may help someone to be a busy old person, but as art and accomplishment it can help him to be fully alive.

What this means in teaching is, first, believing that students such as ours are capable of writing poetry, and of continuing to do it and of getting better at it. It means, too, having the confidence that one can do the teaching. It is, if one is patient and can be free of some wrong ideas about old people, not terribly difficult. Our students liked poetry so much. And some were writing it fairly well after two or three classes. In the conduct of the course, it means always paying attention to the text, and especially to the esthetic qualities of the text, rather than to the person who wrote it. That is, saying, "This line is beautiful. I like the way it repeats the word *green*," rather than, "How wonderful that you could write that." For example, in our class, Mary L. Jackson didn't go from "I had a cat whose name was Minnie" to the lovely music and imagination of her later poems because I thought her Minnie line a "good sign" or because it made me proud, but because I talked to her, in regard to that and other lines about the music in it, the language, the humor. We were never contemplating Mary L. Jackson, she and I, but the things she said and wrote. Teaching poetry as an art meant giving her, always, opportunities to make what she said and wrote better— more inclusive, more intense, more musical. That way, she, any student, accomplishes things. Even when there were apparent setbacks, I kept that artistic, and accomplishing, aim in mind. One trouble with a kind of falsely therapeutic and always-reassuring attitude that it is easy to fall into with old people is the tendency to be satisfied with too little. I could have been "happy with" and "proud of" my students after the first class—even in that first hour, they were better at writing poems than they had ever been. How good it was to keep helping them genuinely to be better at it every time! And how much better than anything I said I felt was their being happy and proud because they wrote well.

Accomplishment was good for our students, as it is for everyone. Poetry must have made a difference to them, too, because the thoughts, memories, and feelings poetry is about are just the things some of them feared they had lost touch with or lost the power to use and to communicate to others. Poetry not only makes people more aware of their feelings and memories but emphasizes their importance. And it provides a way to talk about them that frees one from the usual ways, and that it is a pleasure to hear. Quiet, or ramblingly conversational before, someone who comes to like writing may suddenly feel he has a lot to say, and be eager to say it—

> I'd like to write the book of my life
> I've started it already . . .
>
> Mary L. Jackson

In poetry one can talk about feelings without thinking about the listener's reaction, without worrying too much about looking good, without making anyone else feel bad (guilty, overly concerned) and without the expectation of someone's feeling an obligation to cheer one up. One's feelings, which are such strong things, can, even when they are unhappy feelings, go into making something beautiful, which no one would be distressed to hear—

My husband I loved
He was a good man
He died
He was tall, strong, and a handsome man
He worked hard with his hands
He was sturdy like a tree.

Selena Griffith

7

For the students to accomplish things in an art, the art form has to be within their physical capabilities. Since we used dictation, writing was so for our students. As a form of writing, poetry had certain advantages which helped us teach. One thing about poetry which seems modest enough, but which is very important in this kind of teaching, is that poems can be quite short. They can be composed in an hour, with time, too, for inspiration, reading aloud, and comments—in other words, for the whole cycle of proposal, writing, and response. So each hour is a separate and new experience and has the excitement that goes with being so, while at the same time the hours are really connected, and what one learns is continuous. Students can write a great many works, and works of different kinds, and so get a variety of writing experiences and have many chances for success. One can consider a poem all at once and be aware both of what it says and how it says it—

When I was a little boy and got beaten
It was quiet afterwards.

George Johnson

It is easy, when there is one small subject like this, to talk about it, to give examples of things like it, to cite one's own experience, to sympathize, and to admire its accuracy. Easy, too, to speak usefully about it as a work—to say, for one thing, that I liked its shortness, because it made it seem very solemn and final and silent. It says it was quiet afterwards, and it really is. There are no more words. And that I thought the silent effect was increased by the first line's being longer and having a quick rhythm, while the second is simple and short. From the point of view of the student while he is writing, a short work is less demanding. And the fact that poetry is supposed to be emotional and quick means one can skip such burdensome matters as explanation and setting the scene; one can get to essentials immediately, spontaneously, almost without thought; one can say the best part and then stop. In poetry, one writes about present feelings, and about the past, without needing to adhere to chronology. One can write of past feelings as they are alive in one now—

Spring, when are you showing up?
I like to plant flowers and vegetables.
Summer, when are you coming around?
I like to get out and travel to faraway places . . .

Harry Siegel

The music makes me see soft blues, like the water.
I see small hills that lead down to the water . . .

Margaret Whittaker

Loving a lady could be like a rose
That has soft petals.

                              Eric Carlson

And with its slight formality and its disconnectedness, its
putting things together in unfamiliar ways (three of the
quietest times in my life, comparing someone to many
other things), poetry gives a person a chance to be, surely,
himself, but different from the usual conception of himself (which, for some, may be one who is old or ill or
"finished") and to say things he would not ordinarily be
able to say—

She is like the moonshine
She is like the morning star
She is everything to me
Her eyes are like velvet
Her hair is just like golden grain
Her skin is smooth like silk
Her legs are just like the walk of life
I love her so much.

                              Sam Rainey

The poetry ideas, which helped so much to make learning
poetry possible, didn't seem to limit our students' imagina-
tions. And, when ready to do so, people take off from them
to find new ideas of their own, as William Ross did in

"Storm," for which the suggested idea was "Being the Rain."

> If I was the earth when it rains
> I'd cry for rain . . .

> After a shower you see butterflies,
> Ladybugs, all beautiful little insects,
> And after a shower
> All the crickets go in hiding until dark.
> Then they come out with their music,
> They go into a symphony,
> They stretch and crawl and exercise their bodies,
> They feel so refreshed after beautiful spring rain. . . .

> But in a storm all my earthly neighbors go into
>   hiding. . . .
> They get together and talk about the storm,
> "Isn't this nasty weather we're having?"
> "Yeah, sure is a shame we can't enjoy
> The flowers and grass and all things that surround us.
> Storm makes it too hard for us to walk,
> That's why all of us insects love spring rain the best
> And not storms, which are awful to everyone,
> To all crawling things, to babies, men, and children,
> And all human beings."

8

Writing poetry made our students happier, at least so it seemed to us and so it seemed to the social workers. One would expect it to. The way they were writing, how we and they regarded it, and the value of what they did, made quite a contrast with other activities I had seen or known of in that and other nursing homes. It saddened me, but the contrast also impressed me and gave me the hope that others could see from what we had done what was possible, and desirable, to do in other places.

Soon after the workshop began our students' attitudes toward poetry began to change from hesitancy about it to feeling familiar with it and liking it. A change we could feel was that now we were in a room full of people with a lively interest in something they were doing, which we hadn't had a sense of before.

Students changed in how they talked and wrote. Mary L. Jackson, interested and chatty from the start, talked at first largely about her dreams. I don't know if that is because she thought dreams especially appropriate to poetry or not, but in any case later she began to talk about a variety of things, and to talk well, and to have a strong sense of writing poetry and of being a poet; she said it made her "young again." One thing it gave her, as it gave to all, was a way to talk about life in a way that showed its beauty and its sadness and its humor and, often, because of all that, its value—

> . . . So it was rough
> And sometimes it was sweet . . .
> But I have lived to be ninety-three
> And that's wonderful . . .

I think about Mary L. Jackson, how, when the workshop began, her talking about her experiences and her dreams had a kind of random and rambling quality, as if she were used to talking a lot, saying what came into her head, and nobody necessarily paying too much attention. Later, when she caught on to poetry, she would raise one hand and say, "No, I don't like that line, I don't want it in the poem. I want to say this." It was quite another sense of the quality and of the import of what she was saying, and seemed connected, obviously, to how she was thinking about herself.

William Ross seemed to get a lot of confidence out of the workshop. As well he might have. His was the most dramatic poetic "career" of our sixteen weeks there. Almost every class would reveal some new point he'd reached, some new aspect of his talent. He read books of poetry, wrote and worked on his own poems when we weren't there, and spoke of himself as a poet. These seem modest enough signs, but William Ross had written *nothing* before. One early sign of his natural gift for it was, the first day of writing about flowers, his suddenly being inspired to do a second poem after the first one had been collected. That was his "American Beauties" poem. He often wrote more than one poem in a class after that (as did sometimes Nadya and Mary L. Jackson, among others). William's "I, the Ocean" poem was not only musical, intelligent, witty, and dramatic, but also sustained these qualities over its considerable (and unheard of for the course till then) length of forty-nine lines, beginning

I, the Ocean,
So huge
So powerful
So rich

and moving through considerations of Neptune, mermaids, the sea's cruelty, its calm and beauty, all the things inside the sea, its anger at what humans do to it, and other feelings, concluding

> . . . I hear their laughter
> And I also hear their crying
> And hustle and bustle of the cities
> As I go floating by
> I'm nice and cool
> But the people they suffer from heat
> And I feel sorry for them
> Old cool me.

William originally ended the poem at line twenty-seven, before the part about his (Ocean's) anger at man, then, thinking of that part, called me back immediately to dictate to me the rest of the poem. He had, it was clear, what in French is called *le souffle*, "the breath of inspiration." He read part of that poem aloud, I read the rest after he'd gotten tired, and it was enthusiastically received, with applause. Afterwards there were, among other things, his poem about writing poetry, with its image of "Inner Space," his energetic I Never Told Anybody poems, and his poem about the storm, with its large scope, its dramatizations, and its feelings of identification with small things in nature.

Suzanne, the first social worker, felt from the start that the workshop was doing its participants good. So did Barbara, who spoke to me and wrote to me in some detail about the good effects she observed. We could see this for ourselves, but it was good to have it confirmed. What we noticed in the poems and in the class was apparently going on outside the class also—the students seemed to have more concentration and more confidence. They spoke more clearly and had more to say to us, to the social workers, and to each other. Eagerness to talk about what they thought and felt had replaced reticence, vagueness, and, for some, even silence.

The students' poetry, the center of our attention and the source of all the good things that happened, was sometimes very good. I was often surprised by it. I thought the poems would be about the past, be full of nostalgia and regrets; I perhaps even had an idea there'd be a certain spacious quality and detachment. But I was unprepared for the devastating directness of some of my students' poems, for the sensuousness, for the imaginative and specifically literary power. I was surprised, and moved, at discovering feelings and perceptions in strange perspectives, in lives and situations where I wasn't in the habit of thinking they were. The fact that the poetry was so good, and something genuinely new, made it natural, as the workshop went along, for us to like it, to really like it, and to show the students that we did. This was good for their writing and for our teaching.

One of the best things about their work, I thought, and which seemed to characterize it all along was its unaffected, direct, simple tone, as in these lines about a sea shell—

. . . It's heavy
My whole life is heavy . . .

or these about a childhood recollection of the moon—

> . . . I put out the candle
> But we still had you
> Shining in
> So bright

or these about the end of World War II—

> I was crying and laughing and singing
> And throwing things through the streets
> Throwing things from happiness
> To make a noise! . . .

Sometimes, combined with certain subject matter and with a certain kind of form, as in this poem by Sam Rainey, this quiet directness was very strong—

> The quietest time I ever remember in my life
> Was when they took off my leg.
>
> Another quiet time is when you're with someone
>   you like
> And you're making love.
>
> And when I hit the number and won eight hundred
>   dollars
> That was quiet, very quiet.

That was one fine quality of our students' poetry. Also, as they went on writing, their work became more musical, used more details, was more sensuous and more dramatic. A good example of what they had learned through writing poems is the change from Leroy Burton's pleasant line in the second class collaborative poem (about beauty)—

> The most beautiful thing I ever saw were
> beautiful girls with bikinis on, on Jones
> Beach—

to what he wrote when he took up this subject later, in the last class, in a poem about roses—

> . . . When they are blooming, they are like ladies in
> bikinis
> Lined up on the seashore in the hundreds
> All in different colors
> And a rainbow cloud facing them . . .

Or the change from Fred Richardson's early (fifth lesson) lines about flowers, prosy and informational—"That is yellow/ And in Florida we raise sunflowers"—to his lines in the last class, about the daisy which has "taken in all the beauty of the other flowers." The bright, complex, rich lines by Leroy Burton lack nothing of the modesty and directness of what he wrote before. There is, now, just much more there.

It is probably not so surprising that their work was as it was. They were people from milieus where almost no one wrote poetry, and they had never in their whole lives thought of themselves as poets. They had fifty or more years behind them of not being poets, a rare thing for a poet to have. Many had spent most of their adult lives at jobs like housework, steam-pressing, being a short-order cook. They had unusual (for poetry) lives and were looking at them now in an unusual way (poetically) at an unusual time. It was natural that their experiences would differ, and that the ways they brought them together would differ, from the usual material of poetry. I did think sometimes, too, what a marvelous thing it was for someone, for instance, to be writing poetry, and loving it, who had kept, through decades of hard domestic work, a fine and delicate sensibility that she could now express with eloquence in words.

It seems obvious that many more people like those I taught, as well as those less ill than they, are capable of writing good poems and liking it. Their ability to do so is in most cases restricted by their not knowing about poetry or by their knowing about it in the wrong way, thinking of it as something obligatorily rhyming and abstract and grandiose and far from anything that they could do well. A teacher, of course, can show them what poetry is and show them how close to it they already are.

The problems of this kind of teaching are easily resolved, and the rewards, I found, are enormous. It is not really so astonishing that it all went as it did, and that the students I saw, looking so all alike to me, and so sad, the first day at the American Nursing Home, really did write, and wrote so well. The strength and beauty of what they had to say, once they had said it, made it clear what had been neglected. It is certain that feelings for brightness and multiplicity of color existed in Leroy Burton before he wrote his lines about the roses, and in William Ross the music of his poem about the ocean—

> . . . So huge
> So powerful
> So rich
> I have everything
> Everything my heart desires . . .

These things were in our students but, I suspect, for the most part, hidden. Writing poems, they discovered them and made them into art. They were richer for that, and so, to a different degree, were those who heard their poems and read them. It was not only the details in their poems on the subject of untold secrets that our students had "never told anybody," but all that was best in all they wrote. They hadn't told anybody, and thus nobody had ever heard it, and neither they nor anyone else knew that it was in them to tell it, because they had never written poetry.

The Students' Poems

Childhood Memories and Beautiful Things

AMERICAN NURSING HOME POEM

I remember the national colors of Sweden—yellow and
blue. They hoist them all over the city at all times.
They're flag wavers just like this country. They have
a parade every day in Sweden, when they change the
guard at the Royal Palace—different regiments each
day and everybody goes to see that.

The ocean in the Barbados was very nice—a big wide
sea. We swam in it and bathed in it every day. If you
don't watch the waves, they take you way out to the
ocean. I used to go in every blessèd day as a girl.

Canton—that's all.

I was born in Norfolk, Virginia, and my favorite
experience was going to town on a jitney bus. My
dad bought my first long pants. I was about nine, ten
years old—who knows? I thought I was a big shot when
I had my first pair of pants. They couldn't tell me
anything when I had that first pair of pants. I thought
I was a big deal in that long pair of pants. I thought
I was as big as my father in those pants.

My father was a government doctor and the Marine
Hospital was there and all the men who were injured
in foreign countries. People don't know the foreign
countries paid a dollar a day. The Marine Hospital
was built on sand hills. My father was a great man for

decorating things, and he had beautiful gardens
of flowers.

I lived in Chester, South Carolina. I loved my first dog I
had, Fido, his name was Fido.

I played with a bunch of pets—white rats, birds, rabbits,
and a pet dog. I loved them. I still love them.

Most of my life what I enjoyed most was being on the
farm, even to this day. I played any sport you could
mention.

We had a boy there and he was very poor and we took
him in our house—his name was Heinrich.

The buildings—Betsy Ross, Independence Hall—we were
taken on tours when we were children. I went to a
Quaker school.

I remember going to Morningside Park, my daddy used
to take me every day to feed the squirrels.

I did so much devilment until I didn't know my own
self. I went to bed with my dog.

I grew up on a farm near Vienna in Austria—a place
called Szkalitz. We lived near Hungary, so we had to
speak Hungarian. Our house was international—
Father spoke, Mother spoke Slavic—but we all
understood one another. But now I am an American
citizen—and I'm very proud because I love this country.

I had a teddy bear that I liked. My dad used to take me
to Morningside Park to feed the squirrels. I still like
to feed them. My husband brings feed, and the squirrel
comes to the window.

I had a cat that I raised since it was a kitten. When I would come from church it would run through my legs. When someone killed it, I cried like a baby. My mother said, "What? Are you crying like that over a cat?" But dumb beasts like that, you get to love them.

I had a little dog that I liked. When I was in school I had a lot of little friends that I liked. I was very friendly with the other little girls and I used to have a lot of fun.

I was born in Philadelphia. I used to enjoy skating and different sports. I always wondered about the name of the street, Amber Street. I always thought there must be something to the name Amber. It reminded me of some stone or forest, but I never did know.

Our cat's name was Minnie. She used to catch birds and little rabbits. Our grandmother used to clean them and make them into soup. Once we had measles, the cat thought we needed extra nourishment and brought us more.

by the class

BEAUTIFUL

The locks at Sault Sainte Marie, making air where the ships go through.

The most beautiful thing I ever saw was the flower garden on our farm—the roses, the fruit trees, the cherry tree, all in the springtime. A beautiful sight to see.

The most beautiful thing was the sunset in Washington, D.C.

Well, the most beautiful thing in the Barbados that I was crazy about was the seashore—the sea used to come all the way up to the streets—and it's a real blue water you're getting, beautiful.

Redwood trees I saw in California—their tallness and huge trunks.

I remember the flower gardens on the hospital grounds. There was one large round garden and it had calla lilies—crimson red and white.

I've been all around this country—the Rocky Mountains, California, and I've seen a lot of beautiful things there.

The most beautiful thing I ever saw was my first dollar bill—so I could buy candy for my childhood sweetheart.

As far as I'm concerned, everything was beautiful.

The most beautiful thing I ever saw were beautiful girls with bikinis on, on Jones Beach.

The most beautiful thing I ever saw was my home, the city of Hamburg in Germany.

The most beautiful thing I ever saw was the big Christmas tree when we went to the Pan Am Building. It was the prettiest Christmas tree!

The flowers are very pretty.

The most beautiful thing I ever saw was a rosebush. It was a monthly rosebush—it bloomed every month— every time it bloomed the roses had a different color— there was pink, you know, and yellow, and white.

by the class

Childhood Memories and Beautiful Things

This lesson is discussed at length in the introduction. These are good and easy subjects for first class collaborations though colors, quiet times, secrets (I Never Told Anybody), or quite a few others would work well too.

Colors

All I know is the white sheep
And that I used to watch the collie
Taking the sheep home.
I remember my Communion in my white veil,
And my Confirmation and my marriage.
White is pure.

                    Rose MacMillan

I remember my first blue suit.
I got it before I was twenty-one even though I wasn't
    supposed to.
Everyone was amazed at how sharp I was.

The first dress I bought my wife was pink.
It was the most beautiful thing I ever saw on her.

                    Leroy Burton

RED

When I was very young I remember I loved red.
I think I was influenced by the fact that I was "dark"
And red was becoming.
My mother had me wear quite a lot of red.
It seemed to be such a favorite with my father.
He saw that my Christmas doll was dressed in red.

                    Elsie Dikeman

RED

My brain is red
My dress is red
My hair is red
Lord have mercy on me
The pomegranates in the Barbados are red inside
And sweet
And you know something?
I used to go pick them off the people's trees
But I didn't like them
I picked them just for a joke
And they put me in jail
And they gave me a whipping.

Miriam Sullivan

I like green; I used to see so many greens on the farm.
I used to wear green, and sometimes my mother couldn't
    find me,
Because I was green in the green.

Mary Tkalec

As I remember, blue's my favorite color.
My first date, my childhood sweetheart, wore a blue dress.
And her first serious words to me were I love you.
And that's why I love blue.

William Ross

I liked an in-between blue—I think they call it royal.
Like the shirt Mr. Ross is wearing.
Only more blue than that.
What was nice was to wear a yellow blouse with a blue
  skirt.

Mary L. Jackson

GREEN

Green takes in practically everything:
Green grass, green trees, green money—
Should I say green people?
People who came from Europe are called Greenhorns,
And they've got more intelligence than American people.
They should take lessons from European culture.
Green, green, green, green.
I love green peas.

George Wargo

I LIKE BLUE

All I can think about is I had a beautiful blue dress I
  liked very much.
As it got old I hated to throw it away.
I had a girlfriend who had a blue dress and she saw I
  felt so bad she gave me her dress.
Wherever I went I wore the dress.
And the stepmother was kind of peeved about it.

Peggy Marriott

I remember green money, the blue and green of the ocean.
I remember red plums and cherries and traffic signs
   were red, too.
Red is a very prominent color.
Red is always to the right and green is on the left on
   steamships.

                                    Eric Carlson

I can remember a dress trimmed in silver
And silver slippers
They were fashionable in my day
Blue days
Delphiniums are blue in the garden at home.
The blue breakfast set that was brought to my room when
   I misbehaved
It could have been a half-hour
But it seemed a day.

                                    Helen Lesser

Colors

The poetry idea was Write a poem about colors. If possible, make the whole poem about one color—your favorite color, a color you particularly like. Think of everything you can that has that color, what that color reminds you of. If you like, you can bring in other colors, too. Put the name of a color in every line or so.

The Color Poem was a good simple kind of poetry idea. The subject is appealing; everyone likes colors. Its appeal to emotion is indirect: colors are not overwhelmingly important. Writing about colors, no one feels obliged to have the right feeling. But feelings can surprise one as one writes.

I asked about people's favorite colors, gave examples of colors of a lot of things inside and outside the room, quoted the beginning of Lorca's poem "Romance Sonambulo," "Green, how I want you, green!" and Paul Eluard's "The world is blue like an orange," talked about the Impressionists' ideas about colors—anything I could think of to make the subject exciting.

Taking down individual poems this first time, we did a lot of encouraging and of explaining the unusual kind of writing we were asking for. After all, putting a color in every phrase or sentence is not a usual thing to do. Sometimes the poems begin in a somewhat self-conscious way:

As I remember, blue's my favorite color. . . .

                                        William Ross

and quite often the best parts are at the end—

. . . He saw that my Christmas doll was dressed in
    red.

                    Elsie Dikeman

Such differences between beginning and end show, mainly,
students moving from doubts and hesitations to becoming
absorbed in the subject, so they start to remember things
and to say them.

Quiet

The quietest time I ever remember in my life
Was when they took off my leg.

Another quiet time is when you're with someone
    you like
And you're making love.

And when I hit the number and won eight hundred dollars
That was quiet, very quiet.

Sam Rainey

Sitting alone in a church is the quietest moment in my
    life.
It's so quiet that you can hear your breathing
And your own heart beating.
When you go back home you feel very relieved and happy.

Mary Tkalec

I like to be off by myself.
I never liked a lot of noise.
I was quiet in my childhood, just sitting is quiet.
And nobody around to do a lot of talking.
I used to go off by myself.
Daisies and violets and wild roses are quiet
If I saw them along the road.

Florence Wagner

I always was quiet
And my mother always had to send my sisters into the
  room
To see what made me so quiet.

Fred Richardson

I love it when it's quiet.
Lonely hour in the night it's so quiet
That often I think of things when I was a child.
I think of things my grandmother taught me.
To be honest, thoughtful and to love everybody.
Never to hold malice.

Mary L. Jackson

Mary Zahorjko.
A quiet name.

Mary Zahorjko

When I was a little boy and got beaten
It was quiet afterwards.

George Johnson

Waking up at night looking at the clock.
Waiting for it to go off.
It's the longest quietest time watching the clock go.
Not a sound—just the tick of the clock.

Rose MacMillan

I used to be off by myself.
Anything that doesn't answer you back is quiet.
Clocks, watches, anything.
I repaired them
And put them together and that was it.

Harry Siegel

PLOWBOY

The quietest thing in my life was after plowing acres of
    corn
Then overlooking the work I did and seeing if my row
    was straight.
I was up on the hill with nobody but me then
And no birds making a sound.
Usually after plowing, crows come and pluck the seeds
    out of the ground.
But this time there were no crows.

William Ross

The quietest night I remember
Was going out deep-sea fishing.
Me and my friend were way out on a rowboat fishing.
We caught a lot of fish.
All the stars were shining
The ocean was quiet
The wind was quiet
And we were quiet.
And the fish were biting.

Leroy Burton

Quiet

The poetry idea was Write a poem about the quietest times, or the quietest things, you can think of. You can mention different kinds of quietness in every line or so, or you can make the whole poem about one thing.

I read aloud some poems to give ideas as to how quietness was part of poetry and to suggest various kinds of quietness: the quietness of a scene one sees, the quiet of a room, the quiet of being with people when no one speaks. And the quiet of nature, and the silence one may feel in the presence of something that seems beautiful or important. The poems I read that speak of these kinds of quiet are all short, and I had time to talk about each one: D. H. Lawrence's "The White Horse," William Carlos Williams' "Nantucket," and a haiku by Ryota. This was the first time I read others' poems to the class. I was happy to see how much they got from them. "The White Horse" and the Ryota poem, in particular, seemed to influence both the mood and the music of our students' work.

THE WHITE HORSE

The youth walks up to the white horse to put
   its halter on
and the horse looks at him in silence.
They are so silent they are in another world.

Lawrence's poem suggests a way to make a poem about one brief incident and also makes silence seem a sort of magical thing, at least mysterious. The repeating sounds of *silence*

and *silent* seem part of what makes the poem so final and
quiet. The haiku is mostly a little list of silent things, with
a surprising conclusion:

> No one spoke—
> the host, the guests,
> the white chrysanthemums.

I read this twice (the students liked it), and along with my
localized version of it (No one spoke—/Kate, Suzanne/the
white chairs) it seemed to help students to make poems of
lists of quiet things. It also, with its strangely silent
chrysanthemums, suggested the mystery of a quiet time.
Williams' poem is also mainly a list, of the things in the
room of a Nantucket inn—like the other two short poems,
it has a strong and surprising last line—

NANTUCKET

Flowers through the window
lavender and yellow

changed by white curtains—
Smell of cleanliness—

Sunshine of late afternoon—
On the glass tray

a glass pitcher, the tumbler
turned down, by which

a key is lying—And the
immaculate white bed

I said, "Here are some poems about quietness by some other poets." I didn't speak of them with reverence nor stress distinctions between their own work and that of the poets I read. This isn't bad for a student's judgment but, rather, helps him to see what is good both in his own work and in that of another poet. If a poem by D. H. Lawrence is of another species from his, he is separated by a barrier of "poetic class" from what a great poet writes; he feels (and, I believe, is) less able to come up to what the other has done. Reading poems aloud to students, of which I did a good deal after this, was the best way to help them know poetic literature, since most had physical problems that made it hard for them to read.

Though the quietness idea suggested strong feelings somewhat more than colors did, it didn't ask for them directly. Quietness seems no more important in itself than colors are. There is no strong position to take. The deep emotions silence is connected to are come on by surprise—emotions of times when one was all alone—feeling happy, peaceful, afraid, or overwhelmed.

Leroy's poem, about the beautiful quiet fishing trip, when he "caught a lot of fish./All the stars were shining/ The ocean was quiet . . ." was dictated quickly and surely. He had found his subject and what he would say before we came to take the poem down. This was unusual in these early classes. Many students hadn't yet separated making up a poem from mere conversation. Hearing someone talk very rapidly and randomly about something, we might stop her, as Kate stopped Mary Tkalec, who was talking this time about how quiet it was in church. Kate said, "Yes, that's right, churches are quiet. How do you want me to write that down in your poem?" Mary said, "You write it down, you can express it better than I can," but Kate said, "No, it's your poem, and I like the way you're telling it to me." And "What should I write down?" When it was clear that what was said was being taken down as a line, the student was more concentrated.

Some students did not ramble, but instead could find nothing to say until we talked to them a little. George Johnson said "I can't think of anything . . . not today." Sometimes this meant a student really felt too bad to talk, but usually, and especially in the early classes, it meant he lacked confidence and had a false idea of the kind of thing he was being asked for. One has to talk and make the situation clear. Talk about quiet and one's own experience of it, for example. One of George's difficulties was that he tried to think of something with no noise whatsoever and couldn't. Kate was with him and said that indeed everything did have some noise and that quiet was probably a matter of contrast; she remembered the quiet of walking home from piano lessons when it was just getting dark. George said, "Yes, that's right." Kate said, "I know everything has some noise, but just remember the quietest thing you can." And he remembered the silence after he "got beaten," that was all, but he was very happy with it when Kate read it back to him and when I read it to the class. The people we taught weren't used to the kind of respectfully determined interest in their imaginings and perceptions that we had. It seems possible they weren't used to being listened to that much at all. So it was understandable that we had, at first, to talk, to convince, to reassure, to explain. The dramatic effect of Sam Rainey's poem was due not only to the poetry idea and the poems I read aloud but also to Kate's continuing to ask for one more quiet time. Encouraged to go on, he wrote about three times in his life he hadn't before thought of as being connected.

Lies

I'm thirty-two years old. I don't smoke, I don't drink,
  I don't make love.
I got so damned much money that I can't get a mate.
Damn! I left my pipe in the saloon.
I lived in France and had a wonderful time there
Making acquaintance of the gentlemen.
Rockefeller came this morning and gave me piles of money.
He said, "Mary, you want to build, you want to make
  people happy, Here's the money."

by various poets

I was born in New York City.
But that's a lie—I was born in New Rochelle, New York.
I went out in my blue dress and had a wonderful time.
I used to love to go on the roller coaster at Coney Island.
When I had the blue dress I was in the roller coaster.
And a man's hat flew up in the air and I caught it.
Then he wanted to try to go on the roller coaster again—
With me—and I wouldn't do it.
He got angry and he left me flat.

Peggy Marriott

I lie naturally—no trouble at all!
I tear people apart at every opportunity: It's no trouble
  at all.
And I don't plan to change.

Elsie Dikeman

When I was younger I used to go with a friend to the court.
The police used to bring people in before the judge.
To that judge the truth was a lie and a lie was the truth.

Harry Siegel

I am working hard today.

Mary Zahorjko

All the greatest lovers in the world got nothing on me—
Casanova, Don Juan—they got nothing on me.

William Ross

I'm thirty-two years old. I don't drink, I don't smoke,
   I don't make love.
I dream I have a lot of money and I have the prettiest girl
   in the world.

Sam Rainey

I have a million dollars.
And I have a big estate on Long Island
And five automobiles.

Eric Carlson

I have a million dollars.
I always ride a two-wheeler bike.
A lot of times I wear two pairs of roller skates to get
    around.
A pair on my feet and a pair on my hands.

                                        Margaret Whittaker

I built a great big house with lots of chickens.
With vegetables planted in the front.
Everyone said, "What a beautiful garden:
That's peas and that's corn and that's broccoli."

                                        Mary L. Jackson

I was given something in a dream that wasn't true.
I knew it wasn't true but I looked for it.
When I woke up it wasn't there.
I've so many dreams that weren't true.

                                        Nadya Catalfano

I had a dream that someone gave me a lot of money.
And that's what I can tell you.

                                        Selena Griffith

Take me to the ball game.
I'd like to have a party.

                                        Carmela Pagluca

SCOTLAND

It's a beautiful country
And you don't need any steam or hot water.
The school is right next door to you
And we go by car.
We live in beautiful houses.
We do everything by telephone.
All the men wear berets.
And the police are all very short.

Rose MacMillan

Lies

The poetry idea was Write a poem in which everything you say is a lie. You can make it all one lie about one thing, or you can put a different lie in every line. Everything our students had written so far was about their past and things that really happened in it. The Lie Poem offered a chance to talk about things that had not happened, to express wishes, to exaggerate and be humorous in other ways.

I talked about lies and gave examples: "I'm not here talking to you"; "I'm eight hundred feet tall"; "We are in Persia." I said most lies were in some way true. In a sense it wasn't really I who was talking to them. It was one part or version of myself but not another. If I felt very good I could feel hundreds of feet tall, so that would not be a lie, according to feeling. And in our thoughts or feelings, we could in fact be in some other country. One most interesting way a lie can be true is to be true to one's feelings. I said poetry was full of that kind of lie.

The Lie Poem was a fine idea, but unfortunately I didn't provide the students with something the other poetry ideas had given them: a suggested subject matter. My proposal suggested only a way of treating a subject. Nor did I present them with anything before they wrote that would help put subjects in their minds. I had intended to do that, but forgot to. My intention was to read a Navajo Indian poem which is filled with lies of exaggerated praise. It is called "The War God's Horse Song" and is a poem in praise of a horse—

> . . . The Holy Wind blows through his mane
> His mane is made of rainbows

My horse's ears are made of round corn
My horse's eyes are made of stars . . .

This is a fine example of lies which are true to feelings, and it is a shame I didn't read it, for I think the students could have written good poems of this kind. Later, with the poetry idea of being the ocean, when they were given a new identity to start from, lying presented no problem.

Most of the lies were briefly stated, then left, and their authors seemed detached from them. The poems tended to be short. I was taking down Rose MacMillan's poem that day, and I found a way to help her (she seemed stuck, at first) by suggesting a subject she knew so much about that it gave her a lot of material for enjoyable untrue statements. This was her native country, Scotland. Once she started thinking about Scotland, about its weather, about how the people looked and how they lived when she was a child there, she dictated a poem quickly, smiling, with each true thing she remembered being pleasantly falsified.

Several students were freer and more playful in their writing after this lesson. It was, as I've said, a good idea, which could have been strengthened by more suggestion of what to tell the lies about and of how to tell them—by my having done for the whole class something of what I did for Rose MacMillan.

Flowers

In front of me there sits a plant
With beautiful large green leaves
That feel like velvet
The flower part's color is like a darkish purple
The flowers look like the color of an expensive velvet robe
I know because I often wore the same color robe
And I wear the same color shoes
It's a very soft color.

                              Rose MacMillan

In botany class I had to know all the flowers
The names in Latin and in Swedish too.
The book was called *The Flora*.
I had to press as many as I could get hold of.
And that was in the summertime.
There were some flowers in the winter too.
They grew right through the snow.
The Latin name of it was Primalaveras.

                              Eric Carlson

VIOLET

I love flowers,
I love violets,
They remind me of a wedding,

Everybody's happy.
And it reminds me of the spring of the year
And I think all girls are supposed to have a violet.

Sam Rainey

A cactus flower
You water them every two weeks
A little bit
Little red flowers begin to bloom
And they come from South America
It's a tropical flower
The ground has to be more sandy
I have a book about the cactus
The Christmas cactus blooms at Christmastime
They need not so much water
And the flowers are red
They're like a little bell
There's another one they call an old man's beard.

Carl Koch

There are just two things that flowers remind me of—
Happy days and glad days and sad days.
They remind me of a funeral where they have lovely
    flowers.
And when I see flowers it always reminds me of that day.
And when I go to a wedding with joyous glad music
It always reminds me of the glad days.

Tom O'Neil

That is yellow
And in Florida we raise sunflowers.
And different kinds of birds like sparrows.
Did I tell you about canary birds?
And at night we could hear the mockingbirds whistling.
The birds ate the mulberries
And it made them ossified.
So they fell on the ground drunk.

Fred Richardson

Flowers are blue
And so are you.
But flowers are steadfast.
They never change their color.
They grow in the country
And they're still blue.
I admire them.

Nadya Catalfano

Beautiful flowers in Venezuela.

Carmen Romero

I had three flowers.
A moving man brought them,
They were partly frozen.
We kept planting them
Until they came to life.

One was a rubber plant.
The rubber plant doesn't like water.
The roots like milk.
And to keep the dust off the leaves
You have to use castor oil.
And the other flower was red with little white spots.
A woman offered me twenty-five dollars for it
But I wouldn't let her have it.

Harry Siegel

I DREAM OF FLOWERS

I had a dream that I was riding up the highway in
    Tuxedo Park.
And they have beautiful flowers there
And I always like to stop there and see them and admire
    them.
They had all different colors—
Some were lilies
And some were irises
And they had beautiful tea roses
They were all so pretty, I liked them all.

Peggy Marriott

BOTANICAL GARDENS

My experience with flowers when I went to the botanical
   gardens—
Strolling through the gardens is the most beautiful thing
         for any human eyes to see.
Because flowers are like beautiful people.
I did everything I could to not put my hand on them.
I would like to go back once more
To see if there's anything I missed
Because there are so many beautiful things to see at once.
I know I missed something.

William Ross

FLOWERS

Roses are the stand-out flower among flowers.
They're just like a beautiful woman—
Can't help from being noticed,
Especially American Beauties.

William Ross

Flowers

This day, April 2nd, we brought in flowers. I suggested that the students look at the flowers and say what they reminded them of, what they looked like, how they smelled, how they were to touch, and so on. Just anything the flowers made them think or feel. The flowers, there on the tables—daisies, hyacinths, chrysanthemums, and violets—seemed to delight everyone. We had been inspired to bring them in, unsurprisingly, by the arrival of spring, one of whose signs in New York City is the appearance of flowers in windows and on sidewalks, at grocers and florists. We had noticed also how devoid of flowers and other signs of nature the nursing home was. For poetry, fresh sensations in the presence of fresh flowers might give a new kind of inspiration. Not asked to look back, but to look here, students could write about what they saw and felt right now.

I read aloud some poems about flowers, which showed different ways flowers had been written about: Herrick's "How Roses Came Red," William Carlos Williams's "Queen Anne's Lace," and Rimbaud's "Fleurs" (in English).

Were I to give this class again, I would be sure the students really looked at the flowers awhile, and smelled them, and touched them. They tended to look at them for a second and then go quickly into a memory, and I think I could help them more to be aware of immediate feelings in the present as they observed and sensed the flowers in different ways. The music and touch lessons, which came later, showed how this could be done. It might be good to say, for instance, "Close your eyes. Now open them. What do these look like? What do you think of? Now close your eyes again. Open them. What do these flowers make you think of now?"

There had been so far no comparisons whatsoever in the students' poems. Now, with flowers there to look at, there were some—in Rose's poem and in the two by William. It was only after these first few comparisons appeared that I thought how strange it was that there hadn't been a single one in all the poems about childhood memories, beauty, colors, quietness, and lies.

Music

The music reminds me of a mountain
The mountains of South Carolina
In the wintertime
And it sounds like the wind blowing
Against the house
And the heavy rain blowing on the roof
And now and again with the lightning
And that's what they call the good old wintertime.

Sam Rainey

TWISTED OR TWISTING MARY

This makes my ribs move
I had an accident a couple days ago
I couldn't move
But my ribs are beginning to move
The doctor almost gave me up
Until I heard that music
Then I started to move

Mary Tkalec

Makes me want to take a trip to Europe.
Brings out the feeling to see Europe.
Makes you think of wealthy people with a personal maid
    and secretary.

Makes me think of my friends and wanting to make them
  happy.
At a dinner—something large—dancing and eating
  pheasant
Or riding through Central Park on a warm day.

                                          Mary L. Jackson

The loud music
Makes me think of a fire, with engines
And the color red
I thought I could see flames in the music
I thought I could see people running with a lot of
  excitement
In the music I could see this.

                                          Tom O'Neil

It makes me dream of happiness of people wherever
  they are.
I think there's nothing nicer than getting in a nice
  comfortable chair after a storm
And looking out and seeing beautiful flowers
All different colors.

                                          Peggy Marriott

MUSIC

Reminds me of my childhood
When my dad played the violin to put me to sleep

To dream of a land I hope to live in—
Paradise, Utopia, or Heaven—
Which I am living in now in America—
I am still dreaming.

George Wargo

PICNIC

That music reminds me of a picnic
And it makes me think of my first girlfriend
It makes me think I'm sorry I left her behind

Sam Rainey

It makes me feel relaxed and thoughtful.
The music makes me see soft blues, like the water.
I see small hills that lead down to the water.

Margaret Whittaker

Swinging down the avenue
Dancing, curving
With all them cats looking at me
Hollering "Do it, Miss Mary, do it!"
Curving with all of them cats on my trail.

Mary L. Jackson

HOMETOWN

That reminds me of my hometown
Where everybody works from sunup to sundown
And dances all night and drinks corn liquor
And you have to bring your own girlfriend
You can't dance with nobody else
And it reminds me of a wedding
When the preacher married eight and nine and ten
    people at one time.

                                        Sam Rainey

This music makes me think of dancing
I see pictures
Where I was a young girl and went to the beach
I went with my mother
There were crowds there, dancing at the beach.

                                        Carmela Pagluca

JIGGIN' ROSIE

After being confined
To a wheelchair
For twenty years
I feel like getting up and dancing
All over the place!

                                        Rose MacMillan

JAZZ

The jazz reminded me of Billy Sunday in New York
  in 1924
By subconscious association
Jazz—the twenties—Billy Sunday and the "Sawdust
  Trail"

                         George Wargo

I like the music.
It makes me feel young.
But I'm old.
I like music.
I like everything.

                       Mary Zahorjko

One of my sons is a dancer.
And I would like to be a good dancer myself.
I just feel like I could get up.
But the stroke I've had holds me back.
I'm beginning to weaken.
I've tried hard.
Insist on me not trying.

                    Fred Richardson

Music is part of the soul
Because it makes you think,

It gives you inspiration.
You can't do anything without inspiration.
Music inspires all people
If we didn't have music
It would be like if the birds stopped singing.

George Wargo

Imagination—Big word.
To be Big. You must grow up.
(To Dave) We must love life and people.
We are born by accident.
Die too soon.

George Wargo

WIDOW ROSIE

If I only had legs
And a good man partner
I'd dance the whole night through.
I used to love to dance.
All the big very tall men
Over six feet.
I married one who was over six feet.
And what a dancer he was.
But he's gone anyhow.
I never found another one as good.
Not that I'm looking for anybody.

Rose MacMillan

It gives me a feeling of gladness.
It isn't quite a dance but a movement.
Something that would cause you to move,
If you understand what I mean.
I could get up and do some myself.

                                    Nadya Catalfano

HAPPY HOURS

A wild gathering of people
Like a county election
All drinking and talking at once
In a town hall.

A more quiet crowd.
More jolly though.
I prefer relaxing music.

In a crowd of people in a big place.
Everybody's happy, dancing.
The room is crowded with couples.
With everyone jolly.

                                    Tom O'Neil

A NIGHT OUT ON CHRISTMAS

A jig, a dance,
A fireplace, the fire burning logs
And the tree at the one corner of the room

Decorated with miniature candles
And candy canes.
Because when I look at the candy canes
I think of the fun it is to pass them around to the children.
When they started home, they sang Christmas songs.
And it's a comforting feeling for me.
I sit back in the big chair
And I can hear the voices fading away in the night
As they are getting nearer their homes.

Margaret Whittaker

It makes me think of my childhood days
Take me home
Take me home

Carmela Pagluca

The only thing I can think of is my grandmother's going
        to give me a whipping if I do this or do that.
There was a log house and steps.
I was an only child
And my mother was away working.
And my grandmother took care of me.
I was always expecting a whipping.
My grandmother made me remember that she had
        promised to hit me.
And that was in my head all the time.

Nadya Catalfano

A feeling of loneliness
I'm lonely
I'm missing my family
It makes me think of my family
I miss them very much.

                    Fannie Feldstein

THOUGHTS ABOUT MUSIC AND
ITS EFFECT ON ME

Sounds quiet and soothing
It sounds like all different colors.
Soft music makes me see rivers
Hills, trees, flowers and things like that.
Jazz music doesn't make me feel anything.
I can't relax with it. I can relax with the soft music.
Not with the jazz music.
It makes me think of bells and celebration
And things like that—holidays, parades.

                    Tom O'Neil

It makes me so feel nice inside.
I don't know what it is
But I love to hear it.
Yes, I love to hear music.
Oh, I tried to dance, but I couldn't dance.
My grandmother didn't want me to dance.
But in school I did all the dancing I wanted.

                    Nadya Catalfano

Reminds me of vaudeville or something like that
Clowns and acrobats in a show
Dancing, dancing, and everybody jolly.

Tom O'Neil

Charles and I were ballplayers—
When I was a good dancer—
It makes me feel happy—
Like I could get up on the floor now
And make friends.

Fred Richardson

The music reminds me of a Sunday noon
Home with my family
Especially when I go to the beach
To see or hear the big waves
Rush up on the sand.
And to see all the people
Playing in the sand.
Children building their sandcastles
And the waves wash it away like magic.
And the children don't know what's happened
When the waves wash castles away.
They try the same thing again.
And a little girl cried her heart out.
I, the father, had to explain what happened to her
    sandcastle.
She still cried until Daddy bought her a big ice-cream
    cone
And kissed her tears away.
Then I'm the king of the castle.

William Ross

When I hear New Orleans jazz
I think of the colored people who started it.
They would dance on the streets during the Mardi Gras.
They were singing too.
As long as they were dancing.

Eric Carlson

Inside me any kind of music is all right with me.
Because when I was at home I had a radio.
And I had all kinds of records.
It makes people forget about their troubles and everything.
Music makes me forget my troubles.
For the moment being
Just listening to the music.

Harry Siegel

It makes me think of a lot of young people
Very happy
And having a nice time
Dreaming of the big ice-cream sodas
They would have afterwards.
Taking in a nice show.
Just a dream I guess.

Peggy Marriott

This music reminds me of Old Basin Street
In New Orleans, Louisiana.
There jazz was born.
If you ever go there
All you see is people with some kind of musical
   instrument

Playing some kind of jazz.
Children in the streets
Dancing by the tune of music.
They're either doing the Charleston, or the Old Black
    Bottom.
You even see the youngsters doing the Cakewalk.
And jazz is so fabulous there
They even have jazz at funerals.
Even at churches.
That's where jazz originated—churches.
If you listen to spiritual music
You know where jazz comes from.
That is, if you have a musical ear.

                                    William Ross

I spent most of my childhood living on a farm
Listening to the outdoor sounds like the birds.
On Saturdays we had a barn dance
And all kinds of folks would come to sing and dance
Sometimes we would hitch up the horses and go on a
    hayride.
We would stop to sing songs to the young and old.

                                    Harry Siegel

THE OCEAN

The ocean—
The waves and the beach
It reminds me of my childhood days

                            __   Carmela Pagluca

DREAM

This music reminds me of a multitude of colors
Like petals from flowers floating through the air
Also like a ballet group dancing on the stage
So beautiful
With the leading ballerina with her beauty
It brings out all the beauty of the music and the dancing
I never dreamed that ballet could be so beautiful
Until I saw it with my own eyes
People should be like the ballet dancers
That's what you call beautiful people.

                                        William Ross

MEMORY MUSIC

Music is so sweet
Like turning sadness into gladness
Some sweet music makes me cry
From happiness.
Music charms the savage beast.
It makes me younger than I am
Back to my childhood
And the name of my first boyfriend, Charles,
He played the accordion so beautifully—
So do I.

                                        Rose MacMillan

LOST FRIEND

It talks more silently now
Like to a friend
That they are finished whatever they were doing
It's departure—they go away from each other
They are telling good-bye—till we meet again.
It might be in Eternity
And this is good-bye, dear friend.

Mary Tkalec

Music—First Lesson

In this class we played music on a phonograph. I said,
"Listen to this music and say what it makes you feel, think,
and remember. Do you see any colors when you hear it?
see any scenes? think of anybody or anyplace? Try closing
your eyes and listening. Then write what the music made
you see or feel. Close your eyes again, and see what it
makes you feel this time." The sound of the music we
played was a pleasant surprise to our students. There was
no more music in the nursing home than there were
flowers. Music can have an inspiring effect. I had used
writing to music before with other classes, and I had also
done it myself. Frank O'Hara wrote some splendid poems
this way. Writing "to music" can be a little bit like writing to secret excited feelings, the music being like a physical form of inspiration.

I put on a record (Mozart's Symphonia #40) as soon as
I arrived, and it played while members of the class were
still coming in. After I'd explained the idea, I read a few
poems aloud to show ways music could be talked about in
poetry, such as Shakespeare's song

> Orpheus with his lute made trees,
> And the mountain tops that freeze,
> Bow themselves when he did sing . . .

to give an idea of the magic and marvelous effects music
could have; and a passage from "Song of Myself" about
ordinary sounds that are a kind of music—

> . . . I hear the bravuras of birds . . . the bustle
> of growing wheat . . . gossip of flames . . . clack
> of sticks cooking my meals . . .
>
> The ring of alarm bells . . . the cry of fire . . .
> the whirr of swift-streaking engines and
> horse-carts with premonitory tinkles and
> colored lights,
> The steam whistle . . .
>
> Whitman, "Song of Myself,"
> Section 26

For the writing I put on a new record. I wanted the sound to be fresh and surprising so that their reaction to it might be quicker. So I took off the Mozart and played a record of Baroque music for trumpet and strings—by Vivaldi, Manfredini, and Torelli. It was moving, dark, brassy, and beautiful. I played it fairly loud. With everyone I worked with, I said, "Close your eyes. What does that make you feel or see?" When someone seemed stuck, after a line or two, I said, "Close your eyes again and listen until you hear something else in it."

A lot happened in this class, because the music really turned out to be inspiring. Even more than the flowers, it gave people sensations, moods, and memories just by being there. It was tactile as well as something to hear, and it made the whole body feel things like past movements and moods. This could make people feel transported to other times and scenes, not just remember them.

If a student misunderstood the poetry idea as asking for general statements about music or for an account of his tastes in music, we explained, "No, it is what you see or feel when you listen to the music that the poem should be about. Try that." The music was exciting enough to make doing that quite easy. Sometimes, if a student seemed to feel obliged to always say, "The music reminds me . . ." or "The music makes me feel . . ." we said, "You don't have to say that. You don't have to mention the music at all. Try just saying what it makes you feel."

These poems were written quickly and enthusiastically, and about twenty minutes were left. If William had written two poems in the Flowers class, perhaps this time everyone could. I decided to try for another poem and to use for it another kind of music. I read aloud the first poems and proposed they do another. I played a New Orleans jazz record, Kid Orly and Wilbur de Paris. This music had an even stronger effect than the first—it seemed more directly physical, more charged with feelings of youth and of dancing.

One thing jazz seemed to do was to put everybody in a good mood. Rose wrote her poem with a smile and decided to title it "Jiggin' Rosie." Mary Tkalec had a bad headache at the beginning of the class; then, listening to the Baroque music, she'd written "Lost Friend," which is sad and quiet. As soon as the jazz had been on for a minute, she called me over and told me her wild, funny poem, which she decided to call "Twisted or Twisting Mary," about how the music was healing her ribs (it seemed as though it might have been influenced by Shakespeare's Orpheus poem) .

There was a lot of good poetry in this class, and a lot of excitement. I was struck by how quickly the music changed the students' moods, and by the fact that being so affected, they found it easy to write two poems. The nursing-home students seemed as subject to momentary inspiration as others who write poetry.

Music—Second Lesson

The poetry idea was the same as the time before. What was different were the records and the fact that it was the second time. The surprisingness of the first music class was important, but I wanted to use music again to give more experience in "hearing" inspiration and to offer inspiration in a different mood. I played a record called *Renaissance de la Harpe Celtique*—Celtic harp music, with a high, lonely, sad sort of sound.

Sam Rainey's sad nostalgic poem about a picnic he wrote by closing his eyes and listening, saying a line, then listening again—

> That music reminds me of a picnic
> And it makes me think of my first girlfriend
> It makes me think I'm sorry I left her behind

Like Margaret Whittaker's poem of the time before, about hills leading down to the water, this poem gets one thought or one feeling at a time, just letting them come, one by one, rather than organizing them into a logical syntax, which could greatly diminish their effect. Music seemed to help people write this way.

After the Celtic harp poems were written, I asked for another poem, and put on another record, but this time I believe I chose the wrong one. There wasn't much time left either, and perhaps worst of all, because of that, I didn't read the first poems aloud to them before they wrote the second ones. If the class is going to write two poems in an hour, hearing the first poem makes a good transition and is a good inspiration. The record I played was gospel rock. It was nice and noisy but not exciting and dancy, as the New Orleans jazz had been. Several students said it was hard to write to it because there were words, someone singing, on the record, which distracted them. Not so many students wrote, and the poems that were written seem less inspired than the others written to music.

In these two music classes the students began to be more interested in titles. The excitement, I believe, made finding them pleasanter and easier. The few titles they'd given before were mostly flatly descriptive. In those for the poems to music there was much more variety: "We're All in It," "Widow Rosie," "Twisted or Twisting Mary," "Happy Hours," "Picnic," "The Ocean," "Thoughts About Music and Its Effects on Me," "Winter Time," "Lost Friend." We had more titles from then on.

Many kinds of records can be used to inspire writing, musical records as well as records of sounds, such as the ocean or bird calls. A good way to judge what music to play is to think not so much of what one imagines the students are used to, or will like, as of what one responds to oneself with feeling. Vivaldi and Celtic harp music were unfamiliar to most of my students, but they found them inspiring to write to.

Touch

The gold chain makes me feel like something I'm going
    to DO something with
I turn it around my finger—once, twice—three times is
    too much
The touch is something you glide over till you get to the
    end
But I've twined it around my four fingers
And there is no end to it—
To me it's beautiful.

Nadya Catalfano

ORANGE

It feels cool and soft and round
It feels real nice
Like a snowball
It feels so good
That if I keep feeling it much longer
I'm going to eat it.

Eric Carlson

The Christmas ball reminds me of Christmastime, with
    its decorations
It feels hard and smooth
The sea shell reminds me of going swimming
Taking a dive and finding the shell under the water

The shell is hard, the water was hard too
All salt water is hard
Reminds me of salt air
The velvet ribbon is soft
Makes me think of hairbows tied in people's hair
I used to tie bows in my girlfriend's hair
Feeling soft and affection
It gave me such a thrill
Running fingers through her hair.

Leroy Burton

The sea shell, soft and smooth,
Gives me a relaxed feeling.
The ribbon, grosgrain, gives a rough slidy feeling.
The crinkly lace reminds me of the veil from my
    First Communion.
The Christmas ball is smooth and shiny and hard.

Margaret Whittaker

I had a little dog
He was a miniature pinscher
His name was Tasso
It was a Greek name
It was black and brown fur.
A parrot
They like you to touch them if they know you
He could talk
Always saying "hello" or "you want a cracker"
I made him tame.

He would sit on my shoulder and give me a kiss.
Put his bill on my cheek
He was a cockatoo
He would put his head down
He liked you to scratch his head.

Carl Koch

SUCH FRUIT GROWS IN FLORIDA

This is a lemon the shape of a lemon—this is a valuable
    friend.
This is a lemon, the shape reminds me of when I was a
      baby at my mother's breast.
It has a nice aroma and could be used for many many
    things.
Also it's good for a cold and you can suck on it and get the
    juice of it— You can get cold lemonade when your
    body's warm.
It reminds me of a young girl's breast.
It's smooth, soft, and cool.
It would be good to squeeze in somebody's eye.
This reminds me of Florida.
Walk out in the yard underneath the mango tree
And pick a mango.
This reminds me of mangos more than anything else.
It reminds me of peaches a little bit.
All that combination, it's a good fruit.

Mary Tkalec, William Ross, and
Leroy Burton

POEM

Lace,
It makes me think of a tent
Out in the open where children play
And enjoy themselves
Until their mother calls them to come to eat
And then you hear plenty of laughter and joy
They don't seem to have a worry in the world
These children
They're just thinking of all the goodies Mother has
    waiting for them
They have a tent in the yard where they play
A storm comes up and in the tent they go—
And stay there until it's time to go in.

                                    Peggy Marriott

A string of beads
They feel like pearls
Like a woman wears around her neck
When she goes out to weddings and parties.
They look like wood
And they're hard.

                                    Harry Siegel

Nice and cold and refreshing
The aroma is a smooth fresh lemon
It's a food and also for medication

You can also hit somebody with it
I come from a tough country, a tough town,
And this is good to be protected with.

Mary Tkalec

TOUCH

1.

The feel of this reminds me of a lovely and beautiful
young lady
When I'm making love
So soft, smooth, and nice
That's what a beautiful woman's made of
Softness
And something to hold
If only it was flesh
I love to touch soft things
Everything soft reminds me of a beautiful woman

2.

Reminds me of hardness
Hard, just like the alcohol it stops from leaking the bottles
To me hardness is roughness
You don't get any feeling from hardness
Anything hard feels like cruelty, selfishness, and loneliness.

William Ross

SEA SHELL

The sea shell makes me think of the sea
The waves in the water running against the rock
It makes me wish I was in the water

It makes me feel good to touch and lean back
And think about where it comes from.

Sam Rainey

This powder puff makes me think of your hair
So nice and soft
It's so soft and clean I could feel it all day.

Sam Rainey

It's hard, the Christmas ball.
The lace is pretty, it feels soft.
I like it very much.
I like it very much.
I used to wear a white dress with lace when I was a
    little girl.

Selena Griffith

THE DRINKING CUP YOU DIDN'T PICK UP

A smooth stone
Reminds me when we were kids, we'd go and look for
    stones
And try to find the smoothest
And the rough stones
But this is a soft-feeling stone
We'd go "stone-hunting"
And we would try to find smooth and "sliding" stones
Then we would make something from the stones
We'd collect the smooth ones
We would wade in the brook
And dig for the smooth-feeling ones
And we'd rub our hands on it

We would try to make little cups
We'd make a circle of one round
Then place another round on top of it.
Cups that were like little bowls
And we'd fill it with something cool to drink
But they'd fall apart on us
But we'd get straws and drink it fast
Because the cups would leak.

Margaret Whittaker

"It" reminds me of an oversized "powder puff" and *that* reminds me of an article for women I read some years ago—namely to watch our appearance when we grew old —to make sure we look as attractive as we can at all times. Now that I've reached *very old age,* I find it's a big job, but gives me something to do that's worthwile.

Elsie Dikeman

It feels like a nut
It feels like something prickly
It makes me think of the woods
And the bark of the tree
It's scratchy
It's like life—the things you run into—day to day.

Elsie Dikeman

The lace reminds me of when you have a box of candy
It reminds me also of what ladies wear
It reminds me of my mother
She used to wear lace.

Carl Koch

It makes me think of the seashore
When I used to go with friends and enjoy ourselves
A peaceful pastime
The sound is running out and running light.
I often used to pick the shells up and listen
The sound would remind me of the beach and people
    until we got tired
Then we'd come back.

Tom O'Neil

Dresses
I was about sixteen
It was a party dress
It had bows on it
Small bows
They were soft and pleasant to the touch
To say nothing of how pretty they were on the dress
Velvet
A dress again
Red velvet evening gown
It was exquisite

Helen Lesser

THE CALL

Something soft and gentle
Glides through your fingers
And it seems to grab your hand and lead you
On to something greater
If you only had the sense to follow it.

Nadya Catalfano

Touch

For this class we brought in a variety of things to touch, including sea shells, ribbon, a piece of velvet, a cork, a stone, a lemon, an orange, a Christmas ornament, a gold chain necklace, a feather, and a powder puff. I said, "Touch this and say what it's like, how it makes you feel, what it reminds you of. It might be good to close your eyes and perhaps to pretend that you really don't know what it is you're touching and try to imagine what it is. Write about it the way you did about the music. The poem can be about one thing you touch, or touch something, write about that, then touch something else, and so on."

We placed things on the tables, let students pick out what they wanted, and suggested they touch them as if they didn't know what they were touching. We suggested they touch with their eyes closed; then we asked for associations. What color does it feel like? What time of year? Does it make you think of any scene?

Touch turned out to be extremely evocative, more so than I'd thought, at least as evocative as music. Students closed their eyes and seemed to find it easy to become absorbed in what the touching suggested.

Some of the reactions to this lesson were, not unexpectedly, humorous. Touch has comic possibilities—it is connected to sex and to violence, and also it is not always natural, as Eric Carlson's poem about an orange indicates, to just touch something and take no further steps to possess it. Also funny was the collaborative poem on a lemon which Mary Tkalec, William Ross, and Leroy Burton wrote, after they'd finished their own poems, and other students were still working on theirs. When I read the poems aloud, I said how much I liked the humor in them, as well as the beauty of the associations and the strength of the feelings—all present, for example, in the lines one student wrote about a sea shell—

It's hard to touch
It's heavy
My whole life is heavy . . .

I, The Ocean

I, the Ocean, protect the shells.
I, Mary L. Ocean, had a dream about the ocean,
About these same shells we have here.
I conceal more wealth than land
My fish feed people
My water carries more cargo ships from country to country.

by the class

I AM THE OCEAN, THE OCEAN!

If I were the ocean
I believe I'd feel like a millionaire
Because I'd be surrounded by ocean air
And all the beautiful ships coming and going
I think it's the most wonderful life
A nice clean life
I am the ocean and like to watch the waves I make.

Peggy Marriott

I am the ocean
I feel beautiful
Because I do so many things
I receive all of the dead
And some day I will loose them.

Mary L. Jackson

I, the ocean, on stormy days am always wrecking things
And when I'm quiet and not stormy
I'm singing along with the people on the houseboats
And enjoying the young people swimming in me
Letting the folks fish in me.

Harry Siegel

FLOATING

All those things floating on the water . . .
I'd feel lost
I'd float myself.

George Johnson

OCEANOGRAPHY

1.
I, the ocean, master of ships,
I travel from coast to coast,
Carrying more different people from country to country
I am the ocean, the home of mermaids
Swimming in their castles under me.
I have more company:
All my fish swimming inside me
Also seaweed and shells touch me
So that I am never lonesome.

2.
I also have a terrific temper
When I get mad I sink ships I shake ships
Everyone is afraid of my temper

But I soon cool off
And everyone is happy again
My company is all happy again
All the fish are glad, especially the small ones
Because they are most helpless during the storms.

Rose MacMillan

I, the ocean, protect all the fishes
All the fish are my children
I protect them night and day
And I never sleep
I'm awake all the time.

Sam Rainey

When I came to this country, I came on the ocean
The ship was rocking
They told the passengers to go down
I was watching the ships coming in
We had a storm when I came
And the ship was rocking
They told the passengers to go down
The happiest moment of my life
Was when I saw the ground
My uncle came to take me to this country
If I were the ocean I would be happy to know
I was bringing people to a free country

Fannie Feldstein

I am the ocean
I continue on sleeping
I am asleep
But wide awake
Because I am able to roar
Without a voice

George Wargo

I, the ocean, am known by many names
The Atlantic waves are turbulent, angry
The Pacific, calm, serene
I visit many places
And provide many nations with food
I'm here forever

Helen Lesser

THE LAMENT OF THE SEA

I never realized the big job I had taken on
As the Ocean
Protecting all our sea life and fish life
I know I have to train them
To respect me and respect themselves
So we can make things more beautiful for people
It's a shame the way the people mistreat me
They abuse all the sea life
When they should be protecting it
Trying to make it a better place for everyone

Margaret Whittaker

I, the ocean, have given, and continue to give great pleasure to many. Just *gazing at it* when it is calm, or not so calm, is like a tonic for many. Bathing in it is a thrill for a lot of people, young and old. Boating on it seems like a great and beautiful expedition.

Elsie Dikeman

THE OCEAN

I, the ocean, am a busy place
I transport people to different parts of the world
Different countries
I am mysterious to myself

Tom O'Neil

THE CALL OF THE OCEAN

The waters breaking on the ocean
Splashing around and enjoying themselves
Oh but if you could wade in that
In your bare feet and have them to dash up against you
I would like to be the ocean
Because I would like for everybody to come in it
And do what they want
Things that were never thought of doing, they would do
They'd dance and jump and have a merry time
The ocean would be theirs.

Nadya Catalfano

I am the ocean
I protect the fish
And turtles
And control my ways
Not to be so cruel.

Leroy Burton

I am the ocean
I protect all the vegetable growth
And the fish look to me for protection
Because if they didn't have the water
They couldn't exist
I feel protective toward everything in me
I try to protect all the forms of life—
The shells, the plants, the fish.

Margaret Whittaker

I am powerful
I can rock boats and wreck them
Pounding and breaking
I can be very frightening.

Mary Tkalec

DEEP SEA ME

I, the ocean, have seen all my goldfish
And my very large fish too
I've watched men try to catch fish
They tried to catch my whale
It made me angry
I could have fed them to the whale.

Fred Richardson

I, THE OCEAN

I, the ocean,
So huge
So powerful
So rich
I have everything
Everything my heart desires
From minerals
To all kinds of treasures
I would like to be
Like my uncle, Neptune,
Who's the king of the ocean
And watch all those beautiful mermaids
Go gliding by
Oh how I'd love to touch one of them.
Sometimes I can be very cruel
Wrecking things
That don't belong
In my domain
When I'm angry
All hell breaks loose
Again I can be so beautiful
When I'm calm
I love all the things
That are inside of me
Like all kinds of fish, shells, whatever
That's inside of me, my domain
They all belong to me.
But man
Makes me so angry
By invading my domain
Taking all the beautiful shells,

Gold, whatever they get their hands on.
Just imagine
If you were the sea
And people came in your home
And took things from you
How would you feel?
I bet
You'd get angry and upset too.
What really makes me happy
Is when men, women, and children come to the beach
    and play
I hear their laughter
And I also hear their crying
And hustle and bustle of the cities
As I go floating by
I'm nice and cool
But the people they suffer from heat
And I feel sorry for them
Old cool me.

                              William Ross

I, The Ocean

For this class, insofar as was possible, we brought the ocean to the nursing home—from a Long Island beach I brought a sizeable collection of large clam shells, small reddish-brown-and-white ribbed shells, spiral snail shells, stones, beach glass, three huge horseshoe crab shells complete with pincers, driftwood, four or five kinds of seaweed, and four plastic bags filled with sand. We distributed these things over the tables, for people to look at, smell, and touch, or, in the case of sea shells, even listen to. The poetry idea was Pretend you are the ocean, and write a poem about how you feel and think, and what you do. Tell what it's like, as if the ocean suddenly could speak. I suggested a few things to think about—the ocean in the daytime, at night, when it's cold or hot; the different places you go or are; the things inside you—shells, seaweed, stones, fish, driftwood. Don't write what you think about the ocean or remember about the ocean, but really write it as if you yourself were the ocean. You are the ocean speaking. If you like, begin every line or so with the words "I, the Ocean." I, the Ocean, do this; I, the Ocean, feel that. Before the writing, I read aloud some lines by Whitman about the sea and had the class do a short collaborative poem. They liked what I read from "Song of Myself"—

> You sea! I resign myself to you also. . . . I guess
>   what you mean,
> I behold from the beach your crooked inviting
>   fingers. . . .

Sea of stretched ground-swells!
Sea breathing broad and convulsive breaths!
Sea of the brine of life! Sea of unshoveled and
   always-ready graves!
Howler and scooper of storms! Capricious and
   dainty sea!
I am integral with you . . . I too am of one phase
   and of all phases . . .

Then the collaboration got people started speaking *as*
something instead of talking about it. Short collaborations like this, with me in front of the class and students
offering lines, were always useful when, as this time, the
way of talking was new.

Taking down poems, we concentrated on students' really
getting the personification part ("No, don't say what *it's*
like. Say what *you're* like. *You* are the ocean") and on their
talking about feelings—how it feels to be the ocean, rather
than just listing things the ocean does and places it goes.
"Those sea shells," I would say, "are inside you, and all the
fish. Think of really being that big. How does it feel?"
Doing this, Harry Siegel for the first time went beyond
anecdotal recollection. Kate would interrupt his anecdotes
with "Wait. How would you have felt then if you'd been
the ocean?" Once he got the idea, he dictated his poem
about wrecking things when he was stormy, but when he
was quiet, "singing along with the people on the
houseboats."

What it seemed might be too bold about the Ocean
Poem was in fact what made it so exciting and led to such
good poems. For with this wild idea the students had a

chance to escape from the usual conception of themselves (even more, I think, than they had when stirred by music) and to express, in the new ocean identity, grand and strong feelings—feelings of passion, power, and movement, feelings no less real because those who had them were old or ill.

Talking to the Moon or the Stars

LOVE SONG

Belovèd, I have to adore the earth:
The wind must have had your voice once.
It echoes and sings like you.
The soil must have tasted you once.
It is laden with your scent.
The trees honor you in gold and blush when you pass.
I know why the North Country is frozen.
It has been trying to preserve your memory.
I know why the desert burns with fever.
It wept too long without you.
On hands and knees the ocean begs up the beach
And falls at your feet.
I have to adore the mirror of the earth.
You have taught her well how to be beautiful.

William Ross

Oh beautiful moon
I used to walk for miles and miles
Twelve miles
In your beautiful light
Even early in the morning
Your light is still out
And I still walk in it

Miriam Sullivan

Oh moon and stars
I loved to watch you
When I was a child
I would watch you through my little window
And wonder and worry
What would happen if you got hurt
And next time I'd say
"Oh you're still living!"
To see you hanging up there
Sliding in the sky.
I was happy.
I used to watch you
Through the trees
Then you went down the hills
Until you disappeared
Then I was sad
I wondered again if you'd come again.

Mary Tkalec

Oh moon
You are vast
And your color is silver
You see so much
All-seeing
But you never speak
You light the way for weary travelers
Brightening the way for lovers

Helen Lesser

Oh star
Will you twinkle warmly
And shine brightly

This evening?
So then I know you are traveling
Among your friends.

Margaret Whittaker

I wish I was up there with you
Talking to you
And waiting for the people to come at night
To give them light.

Carmela Pagluca

KALEIDOSCOPE

I feel your vastness
Whenever I look at you
And your beautiful choice of colors
Some colors wouldn't look well
But the colors that we do see are exactly right.

Elsie Dikeman

THE MOONWATCHER

Oh moon, how I want every time that you appear
To just stand there and look at you with eyes glued with
    wonder and awe—
You're so far, far away
But still you appear so bright
Like I was right near you.
When I was young
I used to even talk to the moon myself
About my romances
Because I believed in you.

Rose MacMillan

If I was talking to the moon
I'd say, "How are you?
Is it cold up there?
Are you full of cheese?
(You look like a big cheese.)"

Eric Carlson

STARS AND MOON

You are so far away
You shine like diamonds in the night
You make me think of a time
When I was young and sitting with my boyfriend—
We were holding hands and planning our future
And wishing that the years would go back.

Fannie Feldstein

BRINGING OUT THE MOON

I'm always looking up at you
Wondering if you're ¾, ½, ¼ or full
And whether you've got that circle around you
Which will bring rain.
And when you're clear, you're nice, you're bright
You're shining with the stars and the sky which is blue
And the stars are twinkling right down on you.

Harry Siegel

TALKING TO THE MOON

What a beautiful moon
Dear Moon
I dream of you

George Johnson

STARS

I like to tell them how much I enjoy watching them.
I'd tell them how beautifully they twinkle.

Laura Bradshaw

I talk to the moon
You are a long way from here
I talk to you every day
I see you when you go up
And when you go down

Sam Rainey

Stars, you must shine brighter so I can find my way quicker
I want to go where I can meet you
And tell you my story
Stars, you are bright
I wish I could be with you
So I could be bright like you
I think I want to outshine you
How beautiful you are

Nadya Catalfano

Twinkle Twinkle little star
Oh how I wonder where you are
I wish I were where you are
With the beautiful sky
So bright
Oh I wish I were where you are

                              Mary L. Jackson

Oh beautiful moon
So bright
This night
I wish I were where you are
Oh beautiful moon when you're not there
I wonder and wonder where
Oh how I love you harvest moon
So beautiful and so bright
I remember when I was a little girl and I had to go to sleep
I put out the candle
But we still had you
Shining in
So bright

                              Mary L. Jackson

Talking to the Moon or the Stars

The poetry idea was to write a poem in which you are talking to the moon or to a star or to many stars. To inspire this poem I read and discussed Keats's sonnet "Bright star! Would I were steadfast as thou art."

> Bright star! would I were steadfast as thou art—
>   Not in lone splendour hung aloft the night
> And watching, with eternal lids apart,
>   Like nature's patient, sleepless Eremite,
> The moving waters at their priestlike task
>   Of pure ablution round earth's human shores,
> Or gazing on the new soft-fallen mask
>   Of snow upon the mountains and the moors—
> No—yet still steadfast, still unchangeable,
>   Pillow'd upon my fair love's ripening breast,
> To feel for ever its soft fall and swell,
>   Awake for ever in a sweet unrest,
> Still, still to hear her tender-taken breath,
> And so live ever—or else swoon to death.

I suggested to the class that like Keats they talk seriously to the moon or stars, say how they felt about the heavenly body they spoke to, what they liked about it, what it reminded them of, whether they would like to resemble it in some way. I spent more time on the Keats poem than I had on any poem I had read them before. I wanted our students to feel the beauty (and the influence) not only of its theme but also of its mood, its tone, and its language. The sonnet was a rather extravagant poem to use in the workshop, in being so purely youthful, sensual, and romantic—but extravagant choices had worked well so far. This lesson offered the new rhetorical device of talking directly to nature, as Keats does to the star, Shelley to the West Wind, Byron to the sea, and other poets to other things.

I read the sonnet aloud and talked about it. I talked about its beginning with directly addressing the star, asked them to imagine the scene, the poet in the fields or the street outside, or at his window, thinking about his love, then imagining the star had some quality he wanted. He wanted to be like it, shining steadily, always there, in the same place, always bright. Where he wanted to be was not in the sky, however, but next to his love, with his head on her breast—forever. I said what a strange comparison the whole thing was. And what a nice springlike atmosphere the poem had. Had they ever seriously talked to a star or to the moon? How lovely and sensuous the language was—"Pillowed upon my fair love's ripening breast." Is there anything a star was, or the moon was, that they would really like to be?

In taking down poems we sometimes had to remind people that they should talk to the heavenly body and not talk about it. "Talk to me," Kate or I would say; "I am the moon." There was a striking change when they did, not only in the few words that were different but in the whole mood of what they said, in the tone, in the things they afterward found to say. For example, a descriptive statement about the moon such as "It is a long way from here" becomes "You are a long way from here." This new version is full of suggestions of loving people, of missing them, of all sorts of personal things, and its being so quite naturally affects the mood of what one writes.

For me, as far as teaching goes, the most dramatic thing about this class was my finding that I could use great poetry directly to inspire my students to write. And to write wonderfully well. I didn't have to bring the moon into the nursing home, just Keats's sonnet. The extreme Romantic youthfulness of Keats's sonnet caused no problem. My students expressed youthful feelings easily, and feelings from childhood. In feeling and imagination, there seems to be a way in which a person is all the ages he has been.

Seasons

I love the summer so much
Because I don't have to wear so much clothing
We could never really sleep too much
Because of the music of the windmill roaring in the water
And the streams went under the wheels
The water from the brooks in Austria
Grinding the flour in the mills
At night in the summer

                                        Mary Tkalec

Spring, when are you showing up?
I like to plant flowers and vegetables.
Summer, when are you coming around?
I like to get out and travel to faraway places.
Winter, keep mild, and whenever you're snowing
We hitch up the horse and sleigh and go out
And gather with other people on the farm
Stay out late at night
Singing and the band playing
Fall, I wouldn't mind if you stayed all year round.

                                        Harry Siegel

AUTUMN

Your leaves were yellow
And some of them were darker

And I picked them up
And carried them in the house
And put them in different vases

Your leaves sound different
I couldn't understand why
The leaves at that time of year
Had a rustle about them
And they would drop
At the least little thing
And I would listen
And pick up some of them.

Nadya Catalfano

The sky views are so dependable—always beautiful and different. I am sorry I didn't study them more closely when I was young, but now that I am very old, I shall make it my business to observe them and absorb their beauty to the full.

Elsie Dikeman

I like you, Spring,
Because the flowers start to come out
And the trees are in bloom
In spring the people don't go to bed so early
They stay up and tell stories to each other
Spring, I can't wait until nighttime
Because I like to talk to you.

Carmela Pagluca

SPRINGTIME

Oh Spring, where have you been so long?
I miss you so.
You are the most beautiful season of all
I can do many things in spring.
I can have spring love, spring happiness and spring fever
Most of all, people enjoy Spring
More than any season there is—
The fall has nothing for me at all.
So that's why I love spring.
You'll never catch cold in spring.
Of all the seasons—fall, winter, summer, you are the best.
Some people feel autumn is healthier
But it's not for me.
Give me Spring.
I can go fishing, fruitpicking
Watch Mother put up preserves for nasty old Fall and
    Winter.

                                        William Ross

Summer, you're my favorite
Because you have my birthday

                                        George Johnson

Oh Spring
Your budding leaves are here again
To the fascination of everyone
The rustic winds blowing softly against your face

As you walk among the trees
Are what I like about Spring.
Oh Fall
Your crisp winds
Blow the leaves from the trees
To form a carpet on the earth.

                    Margaret Whittaker

Beautiful Spring
You come with your beautiful violets
And plants so green
I love you!
Now I can wander around
And pick the beautiful flowers
Of the field.
God so loves us
That he sends the beautiful sunshine and rain
To make us happy
And out of pain

                    Mary L. Jackson

SPRINGTIME, HE SAID

Springtime, I love you
And I love to go places and enjoy myself
I like flowers
And trees blooming
And going bus riding
And that's it

                    Miriam Sullivan

Summertime, you are the best season of all
I'm glad when Spring's gone and Winter's gone
And then, Summer, you come in
The best time of the year.
You are nice and warm
We go out and have parties and picnics
And, best of all, baseball games
And when you're gone, I'm sorry,
And can't wait until you come back the next year.

                                    Sam Rainey

It's spring
The world is in love
The trees, blossoms
Spring, I love your rains
The long days are filled with your beauty
The parks are colored with your beauty
The girl and boy are romancing

                                    Helen Lesser

TO MY FAVORITE SEASON: SUMMER

It's the good old summertime
I like everything about you
There are a lot of things I can do in your season
That I can't do in any other
In the summertime I can go to the beaches and swim
But where I come from there's a midnight sun
The sun is out all the time and only goes down for a
    half-hour at night.

                                    Eric Carlson

In the summertime it was warm
And I didn't mind working.
I love to see the flowers and trees grow.
I love everything.

Laura Bradshaw

I love the sunshine
That takes me every bit of the way.
The leaves on the trees turn color.
In Maryland I'd sweep the leaves with my little broom
Sweep them into a big pile
And my grandmother would burn them.
The air is very cool
So sometimes you couldn't feel the heat from the sun.
The air was taking it up.
I always wore my coat
My nose was running
I must have been a sight.

Nadya Catalfano

Seasons

On the same day as the Moon or Stars poems there was time left, and the students were interested and excited. I had my book of Keats with me and decided to read them part of his ode "To Autumn," and to ask them to write a poem in which they talked to a season, as Keats does—

> Season of mists and mellow fruitfulness,
>   Close bosom-friend of the maturing sun,
> Conspiring with him how to load and bless
>   With fruit the vines that round the
>   thatch-eves run:
> To bend with apples the mossed cottage trees
>   And fill all fruit with ripeness to the core;
>   To swell the gourd, and plump the hazel shells
> With a sweet kernel; to set budding more,
> And still more, later flowers for the bees,
> Until they think warm days will never cease,
>   For summer has o'er-brimmed their clammy
>   cells. . . .

It didn't have to be autumn. Spring seemed a likely candidate, since it was now spring. They should speak to the season directly, as if it were a person and could understand them, and tell it what they liked about it, how it made them feel.

Talking to a season is harder than talking to the moon or to the stars. It's easier to talk to someone or something one can see, and spring and autumn aren't as plainly visible as the moon (and my students had no allegorical pictorial tradition, as Keats had, to help them out). They did it, though. One thing that helped, I think, was their just having written a poem to the moon or stars. Two poems on talking to nature turned out to be a good idea.

Simultaneous Events

LOOKING FOR A HOME

Leroy Burton is getting ready for a party.
Gerald Ford is looking for a home for the people of
  Vietnam because they need a home.
They fought hard in this battle but they lost it.
I can see Johns with a bottle in his pocket on the corner
  right now.
Even panhandling for another bottle.
There's a man dancing very fast with a pin-striped suit
  on with the girl in the pink dress.
And, boy, are they swinging.
I see Louis Jordan playing his Mighty Harp.
He's playing "Flying Home."

Leroy Burton

The projectionist used to play punch ball.
The bartender is serving drinks to men and women.
The model is modeling a wedding gown.
The best man's name is Jack, he's in his late thirties.
The name of the movie is *The Gold Rush*
Loew's Avenue B was where the American Nursing Home
  is standing right now.

Harry Siegel

A man is going up the ladder, and he has something
    in his arms.
The birds are so glad to meet each other, chattering
    on a limb.
The man was carrying a ladder, and he had something
    with ashes in it.
The man stopped to write a letter.
I looked down and it was so beautiful on the ground,
    it was summer.
The crow passed by and he was hollering.
A bird came by and stopped and lit on the limb and
    started to whistle.

                        Nadya Catalfano

THE DAY

Kay Medford is making a picture.
Lunches in chic restaurants.
Dresses are being fitted and worn.
Engagements broken.
No explanation.
Gardens are being made ready for the summer.
Muriel Young is preparing for a trip to San Francisco.

                        Helen Lesser

The man in the sweater factory is working on yarn.
The truck driver is stopped at the red light and rolling
    a smoke.
The fire escape is gray and rusty.
The mother has three children playing in the yard.
The dog wants to drink water in the morning.
At night everyone tries to do something for themselves.

                        Nadya Catalfano

TROUBLE

Farmers are breaking up the soil in the farm country
Planting new seeds right now
Getting ready for harvest time
A lot of people are painting their houses
Outside and inside.
My aunt and all her children are doing spring cleaning.
All the girls are putting up preserves
And candy apples peaches cherries apricots
Putting them in jars for the winter.
And the old man puts them in the food cellar.
In court, all kinds of trials are going on
From baby mistreatment and theft
To drugs and what have you.
This is happening all over the world
And not only in the City of New York.
Right now, for instance, people are killing one another.
Father against father, sister against sister.
That's the turmoil the world is in.

William Ross

COMMUTING

Many people at this time are commuting from Grand
    Central Station to Stamford, Connecticut, every day.
The stockbroker is investing his stock.
People are enjoying their jobs on Wall Street.
A lot of women are shopping on a day like this for the
    merchandise advertised in the *Herald Tribune*.
And Sylvia is taking a delicious walk.
But the commuting is what interests me most.

Elsie Dikeman

I went in the woods and there was a nest for some big
  birds.
I put a swing on the old birch tree, the tree where the
  young ones could go and wouldn't fly away.
I took old money from my bank and put it in the candy
  machine.
I took a piece of wire to get the chocolate out of the
  machine without money.
At night, we put a fishhook in the river, and in the
  morning there would be two or three fish.
We were going to make a flower garden in my yard.
At night we stole the flowers from our neighbors and
  planted them in the garden.

Carl Koch

IN THE CLAY MOUNTAINS

I've seen them in the lake, fishing,
And in the clay mountains,
And when the fish come along
Their heads get caught in the nets
Until the men in their rowboats come along
And take out the fish and then sell them to the market.

Fred Richardson

OUT FOR A RIDE

I was taking a ride
As I usually do

To see the sights
And I landed uptown
In the Forties
I noticed
Most of the people
Were all happy
Enjoying themselves
Sometimes I'd meet people
And have something to eat
And drink
And talk about old times
And things that happened
That time
And pass the day like that
It was a relief
To get away
From the regular drill of the day
For a change.

                                    Tom O'Neil

PANAMANIANS

Everybody's cooking.
Everybody's walking and having a good time.
In Panama they are dancing in the streets by the millions.
The men they dance and they get drunk and carry on.
The children are going to church and singing in the choir.
The Panamanians are dancing and singing and carrying on.

                                    Miriam Sullivan

A POEM THAT DOESN'T RHYME

Second-story workers are robbing people.
A drunk is going into a ballroom.
All churchgoers look alike: they've got that pious look.
Everything is going on in Coney Island.
There's no other place quite like it.

Eric Carlson

Kevin and Billy are eating tunafish sandwiches and
   Southern Fried Chicken.
Night is like popcorn popping, or getting the butter
   from Grandma.
The woman on the porch is filling a dish with homemade
   taffy candy.
My mother is pickling Norwegian Salt Berries.

Margaret Whittaker

My aunt lives in Yonkers.
She has a house.
She has a turkey and other animals.
A lady in Italy has a farm.
They grow vegetables.
The lady goes visiting.
She goes to see her daughter.

Carmela Pagluca

We're cleaning the house, the windows, the floors.
I saw the Africans swimming in the river.
I see a beautiful ship coming from the Atlantic Ocean.
In Jamaica and the West Indies we're all playing cricket.
I'm going to Hollywood to get a drink of wine.
We're having a big wedding in Brazil.
It's coming spring now and the bears are coming out of
    the jungle to an open place in the sun.

                                        Mary L. Jackson

Simultaneous Events

The poetry idea was Write a poem about a lot of things going on at the same time. In every line tell about a different thing that's happening. The things can be happening in New York City or all over the world. You can pretend you have some power which lets you be everywhere and see everything that's happening at once. Write about the things as if you are really seeing them happen. Usually in a poem, as in ordinary life, we concentrate on one thing that's happening to ourselves. But even while we do that, we're aware that many different things are going on, inside us and outside. Just think of what's probably going on in New York City while we're here in the poetry class—firemen are rescuing somebody, a woman is having a baby, someone is falling in love, kids are playing baseball, an artist is painting a picture, a doctor is walking through a hospital, a man is let out of prison, a secretary gets her first job. Think about all that and write a poem. Put new things in every line and also be as specific as you can—don't talk about "people" but about "two men in gray overcoats" or "a mother in a blue dress and her five-year-old daughter with long brown hair." Whenever possible, use people's names. The idea was suggested by Whitman, particularly by the long diverse lists in "Song of Myself." After I explained the idea, I read the great list in Part 15 of "Song of Myself," which begins

> The pure contralto sings in the organ loft.
> The carpenter dresses his plank . . . the tongue
> of his foreplane whistles its wild ascending
> lisp.

> The married and unmarried children ride home
> to their thanksgiving dinner . . .
> The pilot seizes the king-pin, he heaves down
> with a strong arm,
> The mate stands braced in the whaleboat, lance
> and harpoon are ready . . .

This was the second time I used poetry as the main inspiration for the writing. In Whitman's freewheeling, disconnected, diverse and strangely unified list I saw various new possibilities for the students' poetry. One was a feeling for writing in a nonsequential way, about a lot of things going on outside and inside oneself—just naming them and listing, not making any connections, not being obliged to find the relevance of an event to one's theme or feeling, but to bring it in just for its own sake, because it is there. It was another way, as being the ocean and talking to the moon were, of escaping from the usual idea of oneself—in this case, oneself as someone who sees only a few things at a time and is in any case concerned with only a few. Writing like Whitman, they could be ubiquitous and godlike, as if the air were speaking, everywhere at once, concerned with everything at once. It was a change of idea about what was relevant that I wished them to get and of what fitted into a poem. I commented on certain of Whitman's lines in which he seems really to be present, seeing and responding to what he describes. I suggested the students do that too—

> The regatta is spread on the bay . . . how the
> white sails sparkle! . . .

I said again, "Imagine you can see what is happening all over the world at this very moment, or all over the country, or all over the city of New York." I had them begin by telling me some lines for a collaboration—

> A man in a top hat is going to church
> People are cooking dinner for a big party in
>   Ozone Park
> And they're going to have a big dance tonight
> Charlie Chaplin is getting drunk he sits in the
>   saloon . . .

Dictating their poems, some students wanted to tell stories, anecdotes about their past that the Whitman passage had brought to mind, and in a few cases where that impulse was very strong, we let that be the poem. But they were missing the experience of simultaneity of things happening, and whenever we could, we found ways to help people put a different event in every line, and with as many details as possible. When they did, there were admirable Whitmanlike effects—the beauty of precise details which made things really "seen"—"a man dancing very fast with a pin-striped suit on"—and the kind of magical life and excitement that came from surprising transitions —"Second-story workers are robbing people./A drunk is going into a ballroom . . ." There was something about regarding each line as an entirely new thing that helped Nadya to make a strangely disconnected and beautiful evocation of a scene. Her poem which begins "A man is going up the ladder" suggested to me another kind of poem to ask people to write, Whitmanlike but all about a single scene or event.

One way to help someone put a new event in every line is to suggest that he think of a new country or part of the world in every line and say what is happening there—as Kate did with Mary L. Jackson.

Comparisons

My husband I loved
He was a good man
He died
He was tall, strong and a handsome man
He worked hard with his hands
He was sturdy like a tree.

Selena Griffith

I loved my home
It was beautiful
In an old-fashioned way
Like a friend
Like an old-fashioned friend.

Mary L. Jackson

MY LOVED ONE

My girlfriend's skin was like the color of a peach
She was soft as lint cotton
Tender and charming like a lamb
Her eyes were like a dove that flies
Her measurements were 36–26–40
And she had beautiful legs, like Mae West.

Leroy Burton

A COLT

I had a mare and when she was foaling
I helped her bring a jet-black pony into the world.
While the mother was in foal, I worried like a father
Worrying about his own newborn baby.
When the mare foaled
I saw the pony's first steps
And she's been my pride and joy ever since.
When she got older, she was my love and joy.
Whenever she saw me
She started snorting and pawing the ground with her hoof
Then ran to me
As if she had arms she could throw around me and hug me.

                                        William Ross

My daughter Geraldine is in Florida
She is like a violet
A beautiful violet
She's like the upper part of the violet
I think about her every night
And I want to go to Florida if I can
To have a home built for her.
My son is the greatest person in the world.
He's named after me.
And whenever he comes to see me
He brings little things.

                                        Fred Richardson

Loving a lady could be like a rose
That has soft petals.

                                    Eric Carlson

Bees steal up on you and sting you
Like birds
And very often leave you the same way.

                                    Nadya Catalfano

The cactus flowers were like bells.
They are like the American Beauty Rose.
Another is like a bell too, with red stars in it.

                                    Carl Koch

BUSINESS 1903–1969 (WITH TIME OUT)

Stenography is like a revelation.
Personal appearance is like a runner-up.
Because unless a stenographer looks as well
As the dictation she's taking
Her stenography is soon forgotten.

                                    Elsie Dikeman

Roses are like the sunshine.
The green plants are green like a green dress.
Petunias are like little angels.
The dogwood blossoms are like little babies.
I water the flowers when there is no rain.
The daisies to me are like beautiful flowers.

Fannie Feldstein

MY GIRL

She is like the moonshine
She is like the morning star
She is everything to me
Her eyes are like velvet
Her hair is just like golden grain
Her skin is smooth like silk
Her legs are just like the walk of life
I love her so much.

Sam Rainey

Comparisons

The poetry idea was Compare things. Begin with something you're interested in and say what it's like. What is it like in your feelings? I wanted to bring comparisons into the students' poems in a conscious and concentrated way, to introduce the words *like* and *as* as regular words to be used, to fix the idea of comparison as part of what one does in a poem. We said to the students, Make the comparisons different from those you've already heard. New ones are better.

I was out of town for this class, and Kate taught it. Before the writing, she talked about comparisons and read aloud an African tribal poem called "The Magnificent Bull," in which a man praises his bull by means of numerous exaggerated comparisons to the most beautiful and powerful things on earth—

> . . . His roar is like the thunder to the Turkish
> cannon on the steep shore.
> My bull is dark like the raincloud in the storm.
> He is like summer and winter.
> Half of him is dark like the storm cloud,
> half of him is light like sunshine.
> His back shines like the morning star . . .

Kate said these comparisons might seem wild, but that they corresponded to the feelings of the poet, and that was what was important, and that is something often done in poetry. To show comparisons of a slightly different kind, Kate had brought some Christmas lights to the class, and while they were flashing red, blue, yellow, and green, she asked people to compare them—to days of the week or to seasons, for example. There was a lot of response. "The blue is like Saturday," "The green is like Wednesday," "The red is like a summer day," "They're like spring; they're like the first day of May, around a Maypole."

When taking down poems, the important thing was to keep mildly insisting on comparisons. Some students started with a comparison, then drifted off into anecdote; others arrived at a comparison only at the end. Unless a student has a strong idea (as William did, and Mary L. Jackson) for a whole poem built around one comparison, it might be good to ask for a comparison and the presence of the word *like* in every line. That assures everyone of more experience in using comparisons.

One good way to give this lesson is to have something exciting and unexpected right there in front of the students for them to look at and compare, as we did later on in the class on Roses.

Writing Poetry

THE BOOK OF MY LIFE

I'd like to write the book of my life
I started it already
My mother died when I was a baby
And my grandmother took over
So it was rough
And sometimes it was sweet
Granny and I, we had a very tough time
Because we were very poor, no money
But I have lived to be ninety-three
And that's wonderful
God has been good to me
I had a shelter and food all my life
Thank God for his blessings to me
For letting me go through all those hardships
And now I'm ninety-three.

Mary L. Jackson

THE DAY

Flowers
Happy things
Clothes
And people
The idea of writing poems
Reminds me of my happy childhood.
I go to the garden every day
And watch the flowers grow

But my roses are really what I like—
One bucket is deep red
The other is a pale delicate pink.
I was thinking when I looked at these roses
Of Kay Medford introducing her pink and red color
    scheme for clothes—
A very chic combination.

                              Helen Lesser

There's a lot of little things that I think about.
I think about them to write them down.
But I don't go do it.
Flowers, I like to see them grow.
I like to see them blossom.
I go and pick them up and put them in books
And save them.
I love to smell them.
I think I hear them.
It seems to me they answer me back.
I watched the bumblebees.
They were bees just the same but they were different.
You'd have to tease them to make them sting you.
They'd sing all the time.

                              Nadya Catalfano

POEMS

I like most all of them I really do
Anything concerning poetry

I've met all these nice people here
I believe that it's good for you to get
   acquainted with them all
It's good to have good friends.

                         Peggy Marriott

I love girls, beautiful girls, girls that model
They're kind and pleasant to be with
And they make you forget your sickness
And they make you happy
I don't have one, I wish I had one
I write about them because they're like angels.

                         Odessa Johnson

POEMS

It's very nice to write them
And read them
You learn a lot from them
What you'd like to know
What other people are doing
If they're in trouble
And if you can help them
That's what I like
To help one another
If we could.
Poetry is very nice to read.

                         Harry Siegel

When somebody else reads poetry
I love them very much.
Since my eyes have gotten bad
I can't read a book or even a letter
But I can hear somebody else reading to me
And I will love it very much.
I like all poetry—
It all goes along.

Fred Richardson

LITTLE MAMIE

When I was a little girl
I played in the yard
All alone.
My brothers and sisters had all gone—
That left me alone.
So I played with the chickens
And the rabbits
And the cats and dogs.

Mary L. Jackson

Writing poems reminds me of my grandmother
She used to tell me things but I've forgotten what she
    told me
She told me about the bumblebees
She said they wouldn't sting me
Writing poems reminds me of the bumblebees playing
    around and making perfume.

Nadya Catalfano

I write poems because I like poetry
Poetry makes me feel good
Just like being on the beach all summer
Looking at the water and the waves coming in
And I like poetry because it makes me think
Of my hometown
Down there I worked all day long
And we danced all night long
The next day we go back to work again.

Sam Rainey

Motherless, fatherless, sisterless,
All gone and no more
I felt so lonely
Yet within me I felt a joy of joyfulness
When I read poems relating to things around me
Like the sun in the skies
It gives me hope for the future.

Mary Zahorjko

I write poems about going to school
And about home and about the old friends
About love and being together with Al
I don't know whether he likes me or not.
I write poems about my brother who does book work
He used to visit me but no more.
I wonder what happened to him
Whether he flies like a bird
And has no time for me.
Luckily I have friends here who care for me
I don't feel lonely.

Laura Bradshaw

A CITY BEAUTIFUL

I'd like to write about the city
That it's beautiful
On account of its parks
And beautiful trees
And flowers
Like tulips
And without trees
The city wouldn't be beautiful.

Carmela Pagluca

Love and beauty
Is what poems should be about.
If you could figure out something about a pleasant
    moment,
Like when I saw my great-grandchild for the first time.
Two and a half years old
That's the first time I saw him.
A two-and-a-half-year-old kid said,
"Grandma, good-bye, I'll see you again."
It made me feel great—
I was in heaven.

Fannie Feldstein

I like the idea of poetry
It gives me a chance to explain my life and my childhood
    days
Because ever since I was five or six years old I was a
    very busy kid
Poetry gives me a chance to go back to when I played
    cowboys and Indians and I shot marbles
I got such a thrill from playing football and baseball
And I'm still a baseball fan today
I often think of Babe Ruth and I wish I could have
    been him
I remember in 1925 when they advertised about his long
    home runs
They were dropping Babe Ruth candy out of parachutes
    from airplanes
We had a lot of fun chasing after the planes to find
    that candy on top of buildings and everywhere
Some we found and some we didn't but we had lots of fun.

                         Leroy Burton

I like sad music
It makes me cry
I like sad poems
Because they seem so true
My own life was pretty sad
I try my best to forget all my sadness
When I have a good cry
It makes me feel better after
To get all the sorrow out of my system
I feel like crying right now.

                         Rose MacMillan

AN ODE TO SOMETHING

I'd like to write about this place
About the people who are in here
And their troubles.
I guess they all have troubles
Or they wouldn't be here.
I would like to write about Fred, my roommate,
Because he's such a nice fellow.

Eric Carlson

INNER SPACE

Poetry makes me feel like I'm among
A lot of friendly people
All kinds
Fat ones skinny ones big ones small ones
A lot of people thrown together
Everyone smiling and laughing—
You never hear violence in poetry
That's what makes poetry beautiful
Especially when I'm at the aquarium
I see all sorts of fish
Everyone going his own way
Peaceful, lovely
Everyone minding his own business
That's what poetry reminds me of.

Poetry is like being in Inner Space
There's no argument or debate about race
For all the inhabitants of Inner Space
Are wonderful creatures—
Color doesn't mean a thing
You find black ones red ones green ones
All is togetherness.

William Ross

Writing Poetry

The poetry idea was Write a poem about writing poetry. I suggested two ways students might want to do it. One, a poem about how poetry made you feel or what it made you think of. Another, a poem about what you wrote poetry about or would like to write it about. Since our students were writing and liking it so much, it seemed a good thing for them to think about and write about—it was a real present phenomenon to contemplate and describe, like spring flowers or Vivaldi or Keats's sonnet, but with the difference that it was something that they themselves were doing. So it was a new kind of object of thought and of inspiration. Writing about poetry might also, like writing about anything, confirm their closeness to it. They might feel even more like poets when they had done it.

I said that writing about poetry might seem strange, but that in fact a lot of poets wrote poems about writing poetry. It was natural enough when you considered how exciting it was, and how moving, and how important it could be in one's life. How could one not write about writing at some time? It was strange, too, how writing poetry was like other things. It could make writers feel the way being in love did, or flying. It could make you feel you were in another place altogether. It could make you feel very happy or very sad. I said I laughed sometimes when I wrote poetry and sometimes cried, and that other poets did, too. No one has ever written a definitive poem about writing poetry, because for one thing there is something mysterious about it, and also it is probably different for everyone who does it. Poets often talked about "inspiration," but no one knew quite what that was. I quoted

Paul Valéry's remark about poetry that it is someone who is not the poet talking to someone who is not the reader. I wanted to say enough about the subject to show in what way it was exciting, to throw out a lot of ideas to help people to think of it as being so. I wanted to get rid of the feeling, if anyone had it, that there was some one thing that was right to say about it, and to show there were many things, that it was as various, individual and wide-open a subject as nature or music. I read aloud and briefly commented on several poems which talk about poetry in different ways. First, Herrick's "Argument for His Booke," a poem that tells what he writes poems about—

I sing of brooks, of blossoms, birds, and bowers
Of April, May, of June, and July flowers.
I sing of Maypoles, hock carts, wassails, wakes
Of bridegrooms, brides, and of their bridal cakes.
I write of youth, of love, and have access
By these to sing of cleanly wantonness.
I sing of dews, of rains, and, piece by piece,
Of balm, of oil, of spice, and ambergris.
I sing of times trans-shifting, and I write
How roses first came red and lilies white.
I write of groves, of twilights, and I sing
The court of Mab and of the fairy king.
I write of hell; I sing (and ever shall)
Of heaven, and hope to have it after all.

I reminded the students of what they had already written about: flowers, music, colors, the moon, and then specific parts of those poems, too: white sheep in Scotland, hitting a lucky number, saying good-bye to a friend. They could include all of those in their poems, along with what they would like to write about now and in the future. As an example of a poem on how writing poetry made someone feel, I read aloud "Autobiographia Litteraria," an ironical but touching poem by Frank O'Hara about being a lonely child and now being a poet—

> When I was a child
> I played by myself in a
> corner of the schoolyard
> all alone.
>
> I hated dolls and I
> hated games, animals were
> not friendly, and birds
> flew away.
>
> If anyone was looking
> for me I hid behind a
> tree and cried out "I am
> an orphan."
>
> And here I am, the
> center of all beauty!
> writing these poems!
> Imagine!

I said that writing poems apparently reminded Frank O'Hara of being a child, and of being lonely; how, in general, writing poetry might make one think of times when one was all alone with one's feelings, sad ones or feelings of exhilaration. I spoke, too, of the contrast in the poem between the unhappy loneliness remembered and the happy, cocky kind of aloneness in the present while writing.

Taking down poems, as always, we asked people to stay on the subject, which for most was easy to do. I wanted them to write about writing poetry, but some wanted to write about hearing it, and if they wanted to do that strongly, they did. Some wrote two poems, one on what they wanted to write about, one on what poetry made them feel.

The students were very pleased with this class, happy to write and enthusiastic about the poems of others. The subject, in fact, was rather festive, giving them a chance to celebrate what had been happening with them and poetry so far.

The End of World War II

I was crying and laughing and singing
And throwing things through the streets
Throwing things from happiness
To make a noise!
The 'church bells were ringing
From happiness!
They were hitting the wash boilers
And people were allowed to shoot off guns
It's impossible to tell it all
Fire bells were ringing
It was like a fire of happiness
Without the fire.

                              Mary Tkalec

I was joyous
Everyone was
People, there was no dividing line
The divisions
They existed then
But for this one day they didn't
We had a little house on Sixty-Third Street
And people telephoned
People called
We were all very very happy
We served supper to all the guests
And this was the war to end all wars
People visited

You went to Chinatown
The restaurants had open house
And dancing in the streets
And then we went to church.

Helen Lesser

HAPPY DAYS

I was at the presses at R.K. Sunshine
Pressing mostly ladies' wear—mostly silk—
Right on Seventh Avenue
Fifteen, eighteen blocks from U
In Washington, D. C.
When the news came over the radio
The girls were teasing me
When I got off the streetcar with my suitcases
They said, "You can go home now—the war's over"
And that night I took the train back to Boston.

Leroy Burton

AFTER THE SECOND WORLD WAR
(WHEN THE PEACE NEWS CAME)

Remember the feelings and actions of New York working
people in NYC? I do.
It was at Fifth Avenue and Fourteenth Street. The office
workers poured out of the buildings in groups—fell
in with other workers already singing dancing crying
PEACE! Strangers hugged each other and cried in
each other's arms.

Elsie Dikeman

About a hundred fifty neighbors gathered together to hear
   the sirens go off
That the war was over.
In two weeks all men women and friends went around
   collecting money for a block party.
We bought drinks and sandwiches.
About fifteen people dressed in costume like cowboys,
   clowns, Uncle Sam, Lincoln.
I was the Indian.
We decorated the streets with lights and flags of all
   countries.
We had four bands playing music from block to block.
The streets were all closed to traffic
And we danced in the street which was so crowded.
I felt so joyful defeating the three other countries,
Germany, Italy, Japan.

Harry Siegel

I was dancing for joy
We celebrated
I called in all my friends
And made a party
There was dancing in the street

Fannie Feldstein

AN ODE TO A DRUNK

When the war ended
I went out and got drunk
I was so happy.

Eric Carlson

END OF WORLD WAR II

I was a seaman
Working, all the time working
Working from New York to Texas
I traveled from New York to Galveston, Texas,
Working for Texaco Oil.
At Forty-seventh Street, the Time Building flashed
The war ended
Traffic stopped
People stopped
Everything stopped
Men were hugging girls
And girls were hugging men
And everyone was happy
There were a lot of tears too.

The ones that are the most happy
Are the ones that had nothing to do with the war.
They care less about what happened
Most of those people today
Have no kind of trade
They are wasteful and criminal
Too bad— If they worked in the Armed Forces
They would have had a trade by now
Being useful to themselves and all concerned.

William Ross

THE END OF THE SECOND WORLD WAR:
TO MY BROTHER JAMES

Friends are coming home
And the sirens are blowing

And they whistle and whistle
Some crying some laughing
And some drunk

                    Mary L. Jackson

I was in New York working for the *American Weekly*
I did a lot of research on the different battles in the war
I was very excited
When we found out any names
We tried to locate the people or their family
They spent a lot of money sending reporters all over to
    cover the story
One gal went off to cover a story
And was missing for three months
But she came home with a series of stories
That's the way we were taught in the newspaper business
To try to live the stories
When the news broke
Newspapers were flying out the window
You should have seen Forty-fifth Street between Second
    and Third
Where the Mirror Building was
They'd take the old rolls off the presses
To roll it onto the street
It was a mess
A madhouse
Actually no harm was done
It was just all exciting
You were bound to find something you liked
Anything from Scotch to Pepsi Cola

                    Margaret Whittaker

THE END OF THE WAR

I just knew that people were coming home
From the World War
And among them were cousins of mine
And they were doing a lot of talking
But I didn't pay much attention to them
Because I thought they were making things up
But later I found out they weren't
Now I know it's the truth
But then I was a child, an only child
And now most of them are dead.

Nadya Catalfano

I was so glad
I didn't know what to do with myself
I was in Panama
I laughed
I was glad it was over
In the wartime I was in Panama
And then after that I left Panama
My husband and I went to Detroit
We lived in Detroit and we had a nice home up there too
After that my husband died
And I was there all alone
And I sold the house we had and I came to New York
So you see I've been in New York ever since then and
   I'm still here.

Miriam Sullivan

No one in my family had to fight
We had enough to eat.
I can't remember where I was when the war ended
I wasn't frightened
Or at least I won't tell about it.

> Selena Griffith

I remember when World War II ended
And I was in Harrisburg, Pennsylvania,
The people all shouting and dancing all along the street
Saying, the war is over and the boys will be coming back
   home
And that night we all went to church
I felt good and I thanked the Lord
I thanked the Lord that I didn't have to go.

> Sam Rainey

WILLIE

Riding on the freight trains
And the boxcars
And singing
They were so happy
That they were coming home.

> Mary L. Jackson

The End of World War II

The poetry idea was Write about the end of World War II—the moment you heard about it, how you felt, what you did, what other people did. What were you doing the exact moment you heard about the end of the war? Were you excited? or what? I gave this subject the same day as the poems on writing poetry. We had extra time and the students were excited—it seemed a good idea to do another poem. Writing about a public and historic event was new for my students, as was thinking about one very specific time in the past. The end of the war seemed a good choice, because it must have been dramatic for all of them, in 1946, when they were in the vigorous years of their lives, when the war, which brought suffering and burdens to everyone, ended. The subject was a way to take pleasure in one's age, to have been old enough then to have known what it was, to really have lived it. Also it was far enough away to be unconnected with any idea of the "right way to feel," unconnected to television and the news, the presence of which would make a purely private response more difficult. I proposed the idea in a way that made personal and specific things inevitable—or almost so—by asking for what they were doing at the exact moment they heard the news.

On this particular day the students' excitement was such that not much preparation was necessary. If I'd started a class with this idea, I'd have thought about bringing in flags, playing records of songs popular at the time, reading poems about war or peace or times of public excitement.

Taking down poems, when a student couldn't at first remember the moment, we asked questions like these:

What time of day was it when you heard? What color dress were you wearing? Where did you have dinner that night? What were other people doing? Whom were you with? What street were you on?

Many of the poems showed feelings of excitement, and these found expression in exclamations and a certain kind of hurried listing and repeating, both uncommon in the students' work so far. Like jazz, the mention of this time made vivid feelings be unexpectedly there. This immediate presence of strong remembered feelings with real durations and real rises and falls helped give strong forms to these poems, which is one of the ways excitement and energy are perceptible in them even when they have a quiet tone.

Mary L. Jackson wrote several poems on this theme and several, this same day, on writing poetry. More and more, for Mary and for other students, being excited about a feeling, an idea, or a memory seemed the occasion for making up a poem. Mary L. had by now developed a very clear sense of her poetic lines. She would dictate one, think, and say, "No, I want it to be like this," and give another version, or change it altogether. Mary L. told Kate that the people she knew back home would think it was crazy to write about the things she did, but that Kate and I were always so encouraging and said it was poetry. Kate said that we were the ones to believe about that, since we were poets.

Reading the poems aloud, I showed how much I liked their drama and excitement. This was a happy day in the workshop. So much interest and so many good poems. Elsie Dikeman stopped me on my way out of the room, putting her hand on my arm and smiling—"My! You really hit on something that time!"

The Depression

BAD THIRTIES

I was born in Chester, South Carolina,
And what I remember about the Depression
Is no money, even if you were working
(And I wasn't working, I was twelve years old)
Meat was rationed and sugar was rationed
And we had a hard time in the Thirties.
And then the President opened the W.P.A.
And that put a lot of men to work.
They weren't making much money
But it got the men off the street,
It gave them something to do.
That was all in the Thirties.

Sam Rainey

MAMIE

The family was very poor
And we had very little
We had to go out and pick up boxes
To make fire
I had no shoes
I had no clothes to wear
I had to go out to look for a job
And one of our neighbors
Dressed me up to go see about the job
I got the job

And I was very frail
It was too much for me
And so finally I got a good one
And I stayed on that job ten years
And then the family faded away
And I had no more home with them.

                              Mary L. Jackson

ME AND MY GIRL

My memory about the Depression is vague
I remember my dad, for one,
Had to go out early cold mornings
To sell apples
To make enough money
To try to feed the family
And I had to help by cutting firewood
And sell it ten cents a basket
I used to go around
Collecting all the fruit baskets I could find
Then I'd cut all the wood
No more than six inches or four inches in length
So it could fit in a coal stove
Sometimes I'd sell, maybe if I'm lucky,
Four or five baskets of wood.
Then I'd slip a dime or two for myself
For candy for me and my girl.
When the Old Man found out
He gives me couple licks
With the razor strap

Didn't do no good
When I see Mary again
Same thing happened
There goes the dime—that's my girl.
You know how childhood sweethearts are—
You cannot conquer love, no matter what.

William Ross

I felt all right in the Depression
I got along fine
I take things as they come
I took it as it came, and got along all right, I guess,
Same as other people,
I'm still alive.

Eric Carlson

I was married.
We had a little house in New York.
145 East Sixty-third Street.
I didn't know anything about poverty.
In the theater they gave benefit performances.
Food was expensive.
Men jumped from windows in the brokerage district.
They were heavily insured.
I was acting in a play.
You grieved but there was so little you could do.

Helen Lesser

I came here in 1928 in the Depression
I remember the Depression but not for me
Because I had a good job in drafts
It was terrible, they were begging in the streets
Selling apples.
I know a man who worked for twelve dollars a week.
They were giving people sandwiches on the street from
   churches
Free meals—they gave them free meals—the Salvation
   Army
They looked awful, the people—depressed.
I was lucky, I never knew the Depression
That's all I can say.

Rose MacMillan

THE DEPRESSION

I was working as usual during the Depression.
I didn't lose my job.
I'm glad to say the Depression didn't make a great dent
   in my life.
I don't remember any great sadness.
It sounds unfeeling but it's the truth.
I can't recall any hard-luck story.
I don't even know if I was married or single.

Elsie Dikeman

I was in New York City during the Depression.
My mother and father used to make whiskey and sell it.
We had a lot of parties

And everyone drank.
There was food too
My mother was a good cook.

                  Margaret Whittaker

I lived at 321 East Eighty-fifth Street during the
    Depression.
Everyone was deprived
But we ate food.
I worked.
We weren't a wealthy family.
There was no liquor.
It didn't really hit me that hard.
I lived with a cousin of mine
And we both got through it.
I worked in Doctors' Hospital.
I did accounting, it was a good job.
I worked there for thirty-three years.

                  Carl Koch

THE DEPRESSION

I had to scuffle and hustle the best I could
A lot of fellows were sitting down and waiting
Had their hand out
I was hustling cardboard for padding
I had a pushcart
And every morning we'd collect the cardboard and
    newspapers
Other people didn't feel like I did

I liked getting up early in the morning—to brace myself
They lay around, waiting for the gift.

Fred Richardson

Oh the Depression was very bad
It hits you so terrible, the Depression
Then when it's better, a little better
You feel so good.
Now you can go on in life, and enjoy yourself a little bit
Now that the Depression isn't here.

Yetta Schmier

IN THE DEPRESSION

You were eating horse meat.

George Johnson

The Depression

The poetry idea was the Depression. We said, write about the Depression, how you felt then, what you did. Both this poetry idea and the next one (on old age) had the disadvantage of being vague and hard to think about. The lessons were useful for our understanding of how what we had been doing actually worked, and of course for suggesting things not to do.

The Depression idea appealed to me because, like the end of World War II, it was a public and historical event that the students had lived through. I had wanted to give them three or four times of writing to music, and it seemed good to give them two times of writing of such events. The trouble with the Depression, as a poetry idea, is that, unlike the end of the war, it is not one dramatic moment. The end of the war was a fact of one's emotional life: one danced, one kissed strangers, one got drunk, one jumped up and down. During a long period like the Depression, one's emotional life goes on in spite of it, even so far as one knows unaffected by it. Something like the Depression affects feelings, but it is sociologists and psychologists who study it who know that, not the persons with the feelings. Poetry about the end of the war asked people to express vivid remembered feelings; poetry about the Depression asked them to try to find some. It required, in fact, a kind of intellectual social-scientific effort that has nothing to do with the way we had been inspiring the students to write. When they thought of the Depression, they mostly thought of the newspapers and of what they heard had happened.

Transcribing poems, I urged students to think of some one particular event, some one thing they did during the

Depression, and to concentrate on that. Once they found an incident, they could write about it, but even then it was mainly flat narration and the giving of information, interesting, and touching, in the poems of Mary L. and William, but not dramatic, nor, like Mary L.'s poem about the soldiers on the trains, moving inevitably along to an end.

Writing on historical events is a good idea, but it is important to see that what will inspire a person to write easily about one is not the mere fact that he has lived through it (or that his age makes us associate him with it) but that it really was a single dramatic event for him. Much better than the Depression as a subject might be the stock market crash of 1929, though I would want to get a sense first whether or not that had in fact been a big event for my students. I might try, because I have strong associations with it, the bombing of Pearl Harbor, or, something less consequential, but startling, the New York City power failure of 1965—if, that is, I had a class of New Yorkers. In some groups, a big snowstorm, or flood, might stir feelings and memories and good writing. A drought might not —like the Depression it is not a single event: the rainstorm that ended it might be better.

Getting Older

LIVING AGAIN

I'm getting older every day
But if I could live my life over again
I would like to travel
I would like to go down to the West Indies Islands
And just lay down on the sand and take it easy
And enjoy life the rest of my life
If I could have my way.

Sam Rainey

OLD PEOPLE

I want to come back as a dove
Innocent, knows nothing about life
That's what I want to come back as
But that's not really me.
A lot of people classify me as a devil.
Even my Casey thinks I'm a devil.
I love old people.
I can sit down and talk with them
And learn more from them than I do from books
Especially older women
Like Mary L.
The old people pet a dove
But the devil they shove away from.

William Ross

I was a young fellow in my teens
I started monkeying around with things
Then one day, my mother, she knew an electrician
She begged him to take me along
I started learning but he let me go
And I was forced to go to an electrical school
Which I do know a little about
I did all kinds of work, handy in all kinds
If I was reborn
I wish I knew then what I know now.

Harry Siegel

There are many things I can't do now.
I'd like to come back again as a person
And live the good life
I love taking care of a family
I love children
I'd have a couple of them
I'd put them to work and enjoy them
Getting old is—I don't know
You can't work any more
It doesn't make me angry
I'm happy about it
I have good friends
That's all right.

Selena Griffith

I don't mind getting older
I accept it as I do the moon and the sun and the universe
I surround myself with young people.

I give parties and go to parties
I don't feel decrepit.
It's there.
What you can't change, accept—
What can you do about it? Nothing.
I just don't think about age.
All youth isn't beauty
Look at the little fellow going to school with his books.
He has his worry and problems.
It's all in the mind.
As you think about it, what can you do?
I think about the good times and the happy days.
I owe life, it doesn't owe me a thing.

                                    Helen Lesser

LIFE

When I was young I was a very nice girl.
And now I am old
And I find myself in a nursing home
But I am still happy here.

                                    Laura Bradshaw

JOBLESS MAN

If I could live my life over
I want to go to an island
Where the sun is hot
And no work to do.

                                    George Johnson

GETTING OLDER

Well, I can't say when you get any older
Things go to pieces
What I mean go to pieces
Is that everything goes wrong
You get nervous
And you get so you can't walk
Now I can't read anything
I want to be happy
And I want to enjoy my family
As they are
But that seems to me
It's impossible
So—I take it as it comes.

Fred Richardson

I'd love to go back to my teen-aged years but I can't
But I'm growing older and there's nothing I can do
   about it
It's nice to be called Grandmother by your grandchildren
That's one thing I do love
I want to forget about my sickness
Old age brought down sickness on me
But being called Grandmother makes me forget about that.

Rose MacMillan

MISSPELLING A NAME

Some people write my name S-E-G-A-L.
But I think that's wrong.

That's like a bird on the ocean looking for the fish.
My name reminds me of "locksmith."
That's my idea of it.

Harry Siegel

I don't like it.
I pray to God.
Praying is the best you can get.
I walk with God.
I love God.
He's all I've got.
God made me.
God loves me.
All the time.

Laura Bradshaw

LONELINESS

I don't mind getting older
But I don't want to get any sicker.
I try to please people—when I'm pleasant
With people, they're pleasant with me.
I don't mind getting older
But I don't want to be alone.
If I can help someone, I do it,
It doesn't pay to be mean.
I don't mind getting older
When people include me in their lives.

Margaret Whittaker

Getting Older

The poetry idea was Write a poem about growing older, either about how you feel about growing old, or a poem like Yeats's "Sailing to Byzantium," in which, being old, you say how you'd like to live your life now, or if you could do it again. I read aloud some poems to the students —William Carlos Williams' "Thought":

> Oh my grey hairs!
> Truly you are as white as plum blossoms!

I read this to encourage a positive feeling about growing old. I thought the ready-made generalities they might get stuck in were about sadness and loss. About this, I was mistaken. More generalities in their poems were about serenity and acceptance—"Old age is a beautiful thing . . ." I talked about my own feelings about growing older. I said I was fifty, spoke of how strange it was to be the same person in my mind, yet a different one outside, how odd to be the same person I was at twelve and at twenty-five, and yet to be so different. Actually, I said, a person lives in a lot of different times at once and is many different ages at once. I feel a loss from being older but also a richness from it, a sense of time and distance and different identities. I think, for all my subtleties, I was guilty in what I said of the unadvisable pedagogical procedure of trying to cheer my students up, to make growing older seem better than I really thought it was. That's no way to help people to write well. I did so, I think, because the topic made me nervous, made me feel I was intruding on them in some way. Still, I thought I ought to give them a topic like that and a chance to talk about such things. I had it in mind to somehow use Yeats's "Sailing to Byzantium." It might interest them by being so angry and so bold about old age and in fact about life. It had in it, too, Yeats's wild idea of coming back to life as a singing metal bird, which might suggest ideas for similar transformations in themselves. I read the poem aloud, explaining as much as I could without the explanations becoming so voluminous they overwhelmed the poem. I talked about Yeats's anger at growing old and his crazy decision to simply go someplace else where everything would be different. I suggested they think about where, if they had infinite power, they would go and what they would like to be. Their poem, if they liked, could be about a voyage, beginning, like Yeats's, with a description of where they are and then a statement of where they're going. I believe I was, in doing all this, fairly eloquent, talking at my best, but it all had little effect on the poems. If the Depression was too vague to think about, old age was equally so, and was, also, which is worse, strongly connected to ideas (and fears) about how one is supposed to feel. The poetry idea, even the fantastic aspects of the Byzantium part, wasn't enough to get through that. The topic seemed burdensome.

So writing about growing old, which I had thought I owed it to my students to have them do, turned out to be more difficult for them and further away from their feelings than writing about colors and flowers or talking to the moon. In those earlier poems there had been very moving evocations of how old age felt—when one student touched the sea shell and found it

> . . . heavy,
> My whole life is heavy . . .

or when another, writing about poetry, felt so joyful about the book of her life. The truth is probably that the most passionate awareness one has of one's changing age comes only at isolated moments (as it came to Yeats walking through a schoolroom), and it's then that it makes one cry, or gasp, or have a vision of what life is about. It is something like the end of World War II. And such moments can't be planned but are come on by surprise, when touching a shell, or listening to music, or writing about something else. They have to be suggested, if at all, as our previous poetry ideas had suggested them, in an indirect way. It's true that the invitation to write a poem like "Sailing to Byzantium" was not a direct invitation to write about age. But I believe our students had been asked so often about age and told so often what to feel about it, that the subject spread a kind of generalizing fog over everything too close to it.

Still, old people and old age—there must be a good way to help them to write about it directly, to say more about what it meant to them to have existed for so long.

I went on thinking about how to do it. I worked for one day in an old-age home in Iowa and tried there an idea that did get something of what I had wanted at the American Nursing Home. I didn't ask for poems directly about growing older, but for poems about a contrast between thoughts or feelings or experiences at one time in a person's life and those in another. I said, "Write something you did or felt at some early time of your life, and after that something you did or felt in a later year. Be very specific and give the exact year, too." This idea gave the chance to put in clear and specific things, strongly remembered, and to feel the contrast between one thing and another—

> When I was nineteen I lived in timber country
>   in northern Wisconsin in a log house ten
>   miles out from town. Two of my four boys
>   were born there.
> I picked wild strawberries and sometimes a roast
>   of deer meat was hung on the clothesline by
>   a neighbor—in the dead of the night.
> By the time I was forty I lived in town—David,
>   Iowa—a very small town. I could see country
>   from my window.
> At sixty—there were grandchildren, but no more
>   wild strawberries.

Addie Reed

This same kind of contrast, inspired by Ezra Pound's "The River Merchant's Wife: A Letter," made the Letter poems, taught later to our students by David Lehman, a very good way to talk about age and time.

I Never Told Anybody

L E A I R

I once had a secret love but I never told anybody
I once ran away but I never told anybody
Once when I was walking down the street
I saw a man running with a gun in his hand
But I never told anybody
Once I found a pocketbook, I was a little girl,
    and I never told anybody
I planted a rosebush at the corner of my house
Every month it had a different-colored rose—a white
    one, a pink one, a red one—
And I never told anybody

Mary L. Jackson

There are things I've even hid from myself
And they're pretty hard to find
My next-to-oldest son, Charles,
He bought me some things.
I'm ashamed to say
I'd put it in the bottom drawer of the commode
And that worried me all night.
Until the next day, when I found it.
You are the only one I've ever told.

Fred Richardson

I never told about the time
I put ten pounds of salt in my mother's sugar barrel.
That particular barrel
Is the barrel she used to make pastries from.
I never told anyone
But she knew it was me
Because I was her naughty boy.
Always doing something wrong.
The reason I never told her
Is because when she hits me
She never knows when to stop.
When I was twenty-five years old
I told her who put the salt in her sugar barrel.
She gave me what-for.
Her mouth was worse than any whiplash in the world.
She's a woman weighing a hundred seventy-five pounds.
Her arm is as big and round as an oak tree.
What a woman!
When it comes to a good whipping
She was the champ.
Because I was always into something.
Once she washed my sister's bloomers.
And put them on the line to dry.
I put a handful of tadpoles
Into the leg of the bloomer
Because the bloomers looked so funny
Flapping in the wind.
Because, at the time she was bigger than I.
She tried to take my mother's place.
When it came to whipping
I could fight her back.
But not my mother.

I got even with her by putting tadpoles in her bloomers.
I never told anyone this.
After she got married,
Oh how I missed my beautiful sister.
I never knew at the time I was jealous of her.
Not because she whipped me
But because she was more beautiful than I.
She whipped me because she loved me.
I'm glad she did.
Because she tamed me off a lot.
I'm still a little mischievous
With people that I love
Especially Casey.
I still have a lot of little boy in me yet.

William Ross

I always told my mother everything
When she was alive
I never held anything back
From anybody
There are feelings, about what aches me
I never tell anyone
They're always asking me
"What's the matter?"
Because they always see me sigh
And not speaking
And I always say
"Nothing."

Harry Siegel

I never told anybody how beautiful the ocean was
I never told my father that I used to go bathing
Because he'd scold me, he'd be afraid I'd drown
I never told anybody the things I used to do at school
But I'm telling them now.

Carmela Pagluca

GAMBLING LUCK

I'd just gotten married in 1930
And I had a job and worked all week
Got paid Saturday night
And I stopped off at the clubroom
And lost my whole week's salary
I wasn't making but eighteen dollars a week, doing
    pressing,
No food, no rent paid
And so my mother-in-law gave me a nickel to get me a
    packet of smoking tobacco
And I walked down on the corner with a friend of mine
And started playing coon can for a nickle
And I won forty cents
I left and went on the railroad men's section
So I got into a skin game
And I won seventy dollars with that forty cents
And I went home and bought food
Paid the rent
Took my wife out to the movies
And my old mother-in-law and wife and all wanted to know
    where I got the money

And I never told anyone
But everybody was happy

                                        Leroy Burton

It's hard for me to tell something I never told
Because I tell everyone everything
I have no secrets
I'm open and aboveboard
I don't keep any secrets
What I've never told anyone is that money is beautiful
The way it's designed and green
Experts are in the line to make it look beautiful
So people won't give it away
Or spend it foolishly
But money is also the source of all the trouble in this world
Money is trouble
People that don't have any money are troubled about it
And people that have money
Are troubled someone will take it away from them
So there's trouble all around
There's always been this trouble
All the wars are over money gained
That's what I never told anyone.

                                        Eric Carlson

HILL

I never told anybody that I drove away in a buggy
I never told anybody that I fell all the way downstairs—
    I'm still crippled today

I never told anybody that I made a lot of pickles
I never told anybody that I sent a letter to the President
I never told anybody that I was in an airplane just flying
around the field

Mary L. Jackson

I've never told anyone this but
I used to go swimming
I never told anyone that I used to go to the store
Because I might go too far
That's what I never told anyone

George Johnson

POEMS

I never told anybody what a grand person Miss Kate Farrell
really is
If it weren't for her I wouldn't come to poetry class
I never told Rainey how I felt about Miss Farrell
Because he's competition to me here
I don't know where he gets his jive poetry from
I never told Casey about how I felt about Miss Farrell
because she wouldn't understand
I never told Casey about my old love affairs because she
wouldn't understand that either
I never told Susan how much I missed her since she left to
take care of her business
I never told Miss Barbara Mittelmark what a beautiful
substitute she is
And that's facts

Anyway, I never tell anybody about my personal feeling
Only to those I really admire
I would never tell Rainey my feelings about Miss Farrell
Like I said, he's my competition
He can't fight me, he's not big enough
I never told Casey that I love her very much
She thinks it's infatuation
I can't tell her that she doesn't know the meaning of the
    word
I never told Casey what a wonderful person she is
I never told my dad that I pushed my sister in the pond
    when we went fishing
I never told Mother that I dumped a whole can of worms
    down her back and ran like hell because she was bigger
    than I
I never told my grandmother that I put turpentine in a
    horse's backside because I was going to church, the old
    horse got stubborn and wouldn't move

William Ross

I never told anybody I used to be knock-kneed
I was knock-kneed until I was twenty years old
I never told anybody about the time I wrecked my
    uncle's car
I took it and wrecked it and never told anybody
I never told anybody about my seventh-grade teacher
I loved her and I dreamed about her every night
I never told anybody about a girl at home
We ran away to North Carolina and stayed there for
    three weeks

They wanted me to marry her and I wouldn't
I never told my wife how much money I made
But now I can tell it.

Sam Rainey

I never told anybody that I wanted to go to school
I never told anybody I was the only child
I never told anybody that I didn't know whether it was
    good or not that I was growing older
I never told anybody that I tried to be good to people.

Laura Bradshaw

I've never told anyone this but
My father used to take me to a dance
For the Knights of Columbus
And I wanted people to ask me to dance
But when they did, I'd say no
Because I'd be afraid, or shy
I was shy then
I was afraid people would laugh at me
I've never told anyone this.

Margaret Whittaker

I'm sitting here and wondering
How many are going to ask me to dance tonight
I wonder should I dance
Because maybe they won't laugh at me
And I could have fun
The steps don't seem to have changed too much
I could still wiggle my feet, I guess
Maybe someone will notice me keeping time with my feet
And will take the hint that I would like to dance.

Margaret Whittaker

I Never Told Anybody

I said, Write a poem which is entirely about things you never told anybody. A poem of secrets. A good idea is to start every line, or every other line, with the words "I never told anybody," and each time put in a different thing you never told. If you want to, use something like a refrain, too, a repeated thing you say two or three times in the poem, like "But I'm telling it now" or "But now I'm saying it." The secrets don't have to be important ones, but can just be things you never talked about because they seemed unimportant or silly or because they made you feel embarrassed or shy. No matter how honest one is, there are always things one never tells anyone, there is always a secret way of thinking about things and looking at things that one keeps to oneself.

The subject, insofar as it was secret feelings, was what they had been writing about from the start: how they felt when they touched a piece of velvet, when they listened to Vivaldi, what they would say to the moon or stars—none of these is part of ordinary conversation or of what one would usually tell anybody. In poetry, secrets can be public and private at the same time.

I talked about some kinds of things one never tells anybody, asked them for examples, gave some of my own. Also, since I thought that their poetry gave examples of various kinds of things one usually never told, I read to them some of their earlier poems. It was the first time I used their own poems to help them get ideas, as I'd used Whitman, Keats, and other poets before. It was a good thing to do.

Taking down the poems, we kept asking that every line or so begin with "I never told anybody." Some students resisted the idea, saying they were honest and open and had always told everything. We said again that the secrets didn't have to be "important" but could be any sort of private, silly, seemingly unimportant things. We gave examples of our own—I never told anybody that I thought I could go inside the radio and sing with the people there. I never told anybody that I talked to my cocker spaniel, Cokey, about my troubles with girls. The most hesitant students ended up by writing about things they hadn't told anyone.

We had been thinking about how to help students individually with their poetry, and we had a few particular things in mind. We wanted to ask Elsie Dikeman to try writing a bit more freely and without such strong prose connections, to talk to Leroy Burton about the endings of his poems, to get Sam Rainey to write longer poems, to help Margaret Whittaker make her poetry less prosy and more dramatic. These last two things we were able to do. Kate, with Sam, noticed that, as he often did, after a few good ideas he became a little nervous and didn't want to write any more. Having decided that was just what would be good for him to do, though, she persisted, telling him it could be unimportant things, and telling him things that she herself had never told anybody. Reinspired by thinking about secret loves, Sam added seven lines to his poem.

I have described earlier the change I suggested to Margaret Whittaker, which worked out so well: that she rewrite her poem about having been shy at a dance as if she were at the dance now and make the poem a kind of talking to herself about her feelings as if in the present. A feeling for writing this way stayed with her in the next class, when she took the part of a rose in a poetic dialogue with Sam Rainey (a violet)—

> ... I feel soft and delicate sitting here watching
> everything ...

I thought of it especially for Margaret, but it seems to me now a good thing to try with many students, perhaps even to use in some way as an idea for the whole class—writing about a past experience as if it were taking place right now.

Roses

ROSES

When I look at a bunch of roses
They make me think of beautiful girls' faces.
I can't take my eyes off them.

Roses are like human beings.
You treat them nice and speak to them every day.
Many people don't believe this but it's so.

My mother had a way to raise roses
The red roses used to get coffee grounds
And the tea leaves used to go on the pink and white roses.

The roses over there are very pink.
And they seem like buds to me.
They're just blooming on, just beginning to come out
To be a large-size flower.

The roses are like pretty girls
Like little tiny girls.

O these roses, how beautiful.
They fascinate me so.
I can wake in the night
And if the candlelight is flickering
I still look at them
With happiness in my heart.

The roses remind me of the blossoming on a woman's
   cheeks.
It's not red and it's not pink.
It's a combination of both.

Darn them! They have nothing to be afraid of—
They just sit up there and look beautiful.

> Rose MacMillan, Carl Koch,
> Mary Tkalec, Fred Richardson,
> Laura Bradshaw, Mary L. Jackson,
> and Margaret Whittaker

ROSES

I see roses as a pleasure, a wonderful wedding day.
I see roses like a carriage coming to take me to a heavenly
    place.

Roses remind me of Nat King Cole's song "Red, Red
    Roses"
Reflects all colors of roses on the street's sides
With sweet smell.

Roses are beautiful like human beings.
We have to feed them so that they don't die.
When they are blooming, they are like ladies in bikinis
Lined up on the seashore in the hundreds
All in different colors
And a rainbow cloud facing them.
The beauty of roses, what else can we say.

> Tom O'Neil, Yetta Schmier,
> and Leroy Burton

They look like people, they get sick like people.
When you don't feed them, they wither up and die.

Give them water so they live.
Don't want them to die.

They look like newborn babies.
They remind me of someone I used to love.

A bouquet of roses on the table.
A beautiful setting for a dinner.
When you walk into a room
Like walking into a nursery full of babies.
They're swaying and laughing to music on the radio.
To me they look like they're smiling and talking to one
    another.

I wish the people could be so good as the roses are nice.

Sam Rainey, Eric Carlson,
Mary L. Jackson, William Ross

I've always liked roses
All kinds of roses.
And my friend bought a house.
He started planting rosebushes along the fence.
When they started growing high, he cut them.
Which was wrong somehow and they died.
And I told him to buy others
So I could show him how to care for them.
Roses always made me happy.
When he planted the others and they grew high
We bent the bushes over and put them back into the
    ground.
They then formed a new rosebush.
They were red roses.
In the fall, we put coffee grounds
Around all the roses to preserve them

And keep them warm and the roots alive.
They bloomed as beautifully the next year.

Harry Siegel

I'm an American Beauty rosebush.
I get one of me put in a vase each morning.

I am a violet. I am just a little violet.
Towards evening I bow my head in prayer.

I am a red geranium.
I love to be watered
And spoken to every day.
I need encouragement to grow
And send off little shoots.

I'm a yellow tulip
A big yellow tulip.
I love to feel the sun on me
Warming me.

I'm a narcissus along the water.
I bend over the water—listening to it!
The water keeps on splashing me.
I never dry off.
But you're the one I depend on.

I'm a daisy.
I feel beautiful in the garden.
I've taken in all the beauty of the rest of the flowers.

Rose MacMillan, Mary Tkalec,
Carl Koch, Laura Bradshaw,
Harry Siegel, and Fred Richardson

RAMBLING ROSE, DEEP-RED ROSE,
THISTLE, PINK ROSE ·

RAMBLING ROSE: I wanted to be planted by the cottage
       wall
      So I could climb up to the mistress'
       window
      And get through the window and tickle
       her chin with my petals.

DEEP-RED ROSE: O Rambling Rose,
      Where you ramble, nobody knows.

THISTLE: I want to sting somebody.

PINK ROSE: Everybody should be like me
      Because this is the way I feel,
      That I'm good to people and I study
       them, how they act.
      If I speak to somebody once that I knew
      I recognize him how he was when he
       was young.
      I'm a personal rose and I recognize
       the people.

RAMBLING ROSE: Are you an American Beauty, or what?

DEEP-RED ROSE: I'm the Red Rose.

RAMBLING ROSE: No. A deep-red rose has got to be an
      American Beauty or a Mrs. Miniver.
      You have thorns. You stick people.

      William Ross, Mary L. Jackson, and
      Eric Carlson

ROSE AND VIOLET

VIOLET: Well, Rose, you're prettier than I am.
That's why you can hold your head up high.

PINK ROSE: I like the fragrance you transmit to everyone.

VIOLET: Well, Rose, I love you and always will love
you.
I'm just strutting and holding my head up
high like you.

PINK ROSE: I feel soft and delicate sitting here watching
everything.

VIOLET: Well, Rose, as long as I look at you and wait
I wish you were mine.
So let's get married and get it all over with.

PINK ROSE: No. You can't mix a violet and a rose.
We'd never be able to have childen.

VIOLET: Well, that's very sad, but I still love you.

Sam Rainey and
Margaret Whittaker

CARNATION VS. LILY OF THE VALLEY

CARNATION: I am a carnation full of beauty.
Lily of the Valley, don't you think I can look good
On your breast or lapel?

LILY: Carnation, I am already in love with tulip flower.
He is beautiful and full of love.

CARNATION: Lily, Tulip will wither and die,
But I, Carnation, will live forever,
And I am suitable for different occasions.

Yetta Schmier and
Leroy Burton

Summertime
exotic
a fire
magnificent
a white boat
love
mystified
Christmas
Pick them
good
bouquet

by the class

Roses

There were three poetry ideas this day, all having to do with a dozen small pink roses we brought in: two kinds of collaborative poem and a play. All the writing was dramatic, with people responding to each other and each other's lines, even in the collaborations. The first poetry idea was a new kind of collaborative poem, of which the dozen roses were the subject. The roses were in the middle of the table, with everyone seated around it. I said, "Look at the roses and say what they look like to you, or what they make you think or feel. Really look at them, as if you were seeing them for the first time. Each person will tell me one or two lines about how the roses look to him. When I get the first lines, I'll read them aloud to the next person, and to everybody else. And so on. So that when you write your lines you'll have heard already what the others have said. So you can inspire each other, disagree with each other, give each other ideas, since you'll be hearing each other's lines." To show how such a collaboration worked, I read aloud, and talked about, an eighth-century Chinese collaborative poem by five poets called "A Garland of Roses."

A GARLAND OF ROSES

Like brocade flushed with sunset color,
Following the spring, they open at summer's touch.

Waves of pink weave shadows that catch our eyes;
A gentle wind carries the fragrance hither.

They take their place beside the eastern pavilion;
Before the stairs salute the upper terrace.

Pale or dark in hue, each has perfect shape;
The buds in secret urge each other to blossom.

We mourn the falling petals that cover the ground,
By the embankment lament the oars returning.

The fragrance is heavy, moist with rain and dew;
The bright vision stands apart from worldly dust.

Their faces are bright as if with rouge,
Sharp cut, as by a clever housewife's shears.

What to do? the flowers leave me no other plans;
I have only these last few cups of wine.

> by Liu Yü-Hsi, P'ei Tu,
> Hsing Shih, Po Chü-i,
> and Chang Chi
> —translated by Donald Keene

It was a common practice, I said, for Chinese poets (as for Japanese) to write poems together. For this poem, the five Chinese poets apparently all sat looking, as the students were now looking, at a bunch of roses, and each wrote lines about them, one poet after another, each having heard what those before him had said. The collaborative poems of the first class were in fact a putting together of individual statements connected only by their subject matter. This time the writers influenced each other's lines.

This kind of poem, with people responding to each other as well as to the subject, is good for a class in which there aren't enough people to take down poems—if you're teaching alone, for example. But in any circumstance, it's an exciting and enjoyable way of writing a poem. I wanted, especially toward the end of my work in the home, to make poetry writing seem as festive and happy a thing as possible. I also hoped to give our students some ideas about how they might write poems together without a special poetry teacher. I really liked in the first "Roses" poem Laura Bradshaw's sweet and funny modification of her first observation—the roses weren't like just any pretty girls but like "little tiny" ones; Mary L. Jackson's bringing together past and present, seeing roses now, and in the past in candlelight, and being so moved by them; and Margaret Whittaker's precision about just what part of a woman's face the roses were like, and then her sharp and touching envy of them.

After three of us had taken down collaborative poems of this kind, I proposed a play, in which each student would take the role of a kind of flower. I wanted everyone to have, as before, in being the ocean, the experience of being something else. And this time in a social situation. And the play was more of a way of writing together and suggested more reaction and response even than the collaborations. In a play, one character doesn't usually continue or refine what another character says, but answers it. Again, with this I hoped to add to the feeling the workshop members had of being poets together and feeling poetry a natural (and social) thing to do. The two-character plays were the most dramatic, both funny and touching little love dramas.

I found this class very moving, since it was the last one, and the students seemed so pleased and were writing so well. It was partly because I didn't want it to stop that I proposed one more work, a class collaboration, when we were already past time for the workshop to end and some students were being wheeled out of the room. "Stop, listen," I said, and read aloud William Carlos Williams's poem "The Locust Tree in Flower." It is a poem all in lines of one word, with each word like a sort of separate look at the subject, and not really making much sense syntactically—

> Among
> of
> green
>
> stiff
> old
> bright
>
> broken
> branch
> come
>
> white
> sweet
> May
>
> again

I suggested something a little more disconnected. I said, "Look at the roses and just think of one word. It doesn't have to have anything to do with roses, really. Just let the roses make you think of a word." Our students, so shy and hesitant about saying anything at the beginning, by now, after four months of poetry, were quick to respond to this odd (in an ordinary sense) but interesting (poetically) request, and eleven of them who were still in the poetry room made up the last poem in this section.

Poems from Other Workshops

Our last poetry class at the American Nursing Home was this lesson on the Roses. Afterwards both Kate and I were leaving New York City. But everyone was still learning. No matter where we had stopped, it would have been in the middle. I thought it would be sad and wasteful if the workshop ended, so I had asked other poets to come to a few classes, hoping that one of them would like to continue it. David Lehman did, and gave classes on through most of the summer. In August I worked for one day in the Lutheran Old Age Home in Cedar Falls, Iowa. The poems which follow from David Lehman's classes and those from Iowa will, I hope, suggest that it is not only with one particular teacher that old and ill people can be helped to write so well, nor only in one place.

Poems from the American Nursing Home in Workshops Taught by David Lehman, June–July 1975

David Lehman taught as we did, with poetry ideas, and usually reading poems aloud before the students wrote. The poetry ideas for classes in which these poems were written are Letter Poems, Poems About a Personal Paradise, Marriage Poems, Poems of Thanks, Political Poems, Being the Rain, Poems Written Listening to Music (Gershwin's *Rhapsody in Blue*), Poems About Fear. For the Letter Poem lesson, David read aloud Ezra Pound's "The River Merchant's Wife—A Letter."

TO JULIUS

Remember when we went to school together
In Boston, Massachusetts?
I used to pop the teacher with paper clips
(We called them cotter-pins)
Shot from a rubber band—
He looked like he was fighting off mosquitoes!
You laughed so hard you had to be taken to a doctor,
And now I haven't seen you since 1938,
Or heard from you since 1940.
I wish I could get in touch with you,
Since I lost my sight in 1970.

Leroy Burton

Rosalind, I want to talk to you about our old-time
     friendship,
I want to hear how the children are doing—
Jerry and Kenneth must be almost grown men now!
Please say hello to both of them for me.
As you know, I almost raised those boys as my own—
They are good friends of mine, just like you.
I hope they haven't forgotten me after all these years.
I would like you to remind them of me.

Please at least keep in touch with me,
If I can't see you,
But seeing you is the best, my dear friend.

                                        William Ross

TO MY HUSBAND FRANK

Honey dear, I want to tell you
How much I am lonely.
I am living by some friends
They treat me very good but
Not as how you would treat me.
Sweetheart dear, I wish you would
Come on home soon. Love, Mary.

                                        Mary Tkalec

TO MY MOTHER

I hope you're better than you were
The last time I saw you. I wish you were alive,
Because I want to go out

And my cousins won't let me.
I wish you were alive.

Laura Bradshaw

Dear Tom,

A desire to write you has possessed me lately
again.

You were eleven years old, and I "about
2 *days old*," when they introduced us. You fell in love
with me at once.

Remember all the years you came on Sunday
nights with your mother (who was *my* mother's girlhood
friend) to visit *my mother, my older sister, and me*.

You may not be alive, but I hope you are and
have been the happy man you deserved to be.

Remember the trips to the theaters, which I
loved, and Christmas Eve refreshments at my house
after the show.

And the piano playing and very poor singing
by all three of us after laughter and talk!

They were *happy, young* times. You and I both
enjoyed them. Perhaps we should have married.

Elsie

Elsie Dikeman

A LETTER TO AN OLD FRIEND

We've known each other all our lives,
And now you have passed,

And I am still alive.
Susie, I loved you so much better
Than any friend I ever had.
When your mother died she left seven little children
That you had to raise. Do you remember
How I used to cook and help to feed them?
Now all the old-timers are gone,
And I'm left here alone.
Oh how I wish you were here, so we could have
A long talk and go to church together again.
Love, Mary.

                                    Mary L. Jackson

FRIENDSHIP

We were friends, that's all we were.
I thought of you and I thought I'd write
to see what you were doing.
I thought that by corresponding
we could tell each other whatever we felt.

You lived next door to me, and you went away
and I missed you. We used to read together, right here.
It wasn't a love affair
but you lived near me and I could talk to you, little secrets.
I'll leave it open to you to answer me.
I'd love to hear from you
So I can tell you my secrets, if I have any.
Right now I don't have any.   Nadya.

                                    Nadya Catalfano

I want to be on a ship riding slowly along
With a nice jazz band playing in the background
Or with Leonard Bernstein's music low like the waves
(His music and the waves at the same time)
With a pretty girl at my side

I want to take a cruise around the world
Especially if we sail under the stars
With the most gorgeous girls I've ever seen

Mary L. Jackson, George Johnson,
and William Ross

MY ISLAND

I would like my island to be a log cabin,
A duplicate of Abraham Lincoln's log cabin,
Where I could write poetry and be secluded from
    everyone,
Where I could think and concentrate on writing
Beautiful poetry, and listen to beautiful music,
And do lovely painting. That's my island!
That's my island of thought!

William Ross

JOHN ISLAND

I'd like to be on John Island
I'd get some billy goats
A team of brown and white, and black and white goats
I'd like to raise goats

I'd like to hear jazz songs like
"Let Me Call You Sweetheart"
And "Ragtime"

I'd like to eat rabbit
With rice and corn bread
And I'd like to drink Scotch

George Johnson

THINKING HIGH

If I could get the money
I'd fly away from here right away
To a beautiful island, where there'd be flowers and
    birds—
I'd eat pheasant
And all kinds of fruit—
Ambrosia—with oranges and coconut in a pretty dish.
I'd go to the ocean in the morning to see the sun rise,
And in the evening I will watch the sun set.
Two sweet children would be there—
Two kind, beautiful children for my companions—
We'd walk on the beach and talk to these children.
I'd have beautiful robes on
And there would be soft candlelight
Flickering in the room.

Mary L. Jackson

I'd like to go to North Carolina,
and once I was there, I'd go out on the town.
I'd give a dance! In the moonlight!
I'd drink anything! I'd see my friends!
I'd see my brother Willie!
He'd be dancing with his girlfriend, Leslie!
All our people would be there dancing! My friends!

Laura Bradshaw

WILLY

How well I remember!
I never will forget
That wedding day
The most wonderful day of my life,
A Sunday
I strolled down the aisle.

And when my husband died
They had the funeral all day.
We were good people in the South in those days
Parents were real strict in the South.
There was so much
And I was so young,
I had it all fixed up,
We were always very happy.

He was a fireman on the railroad.
He fired the engine.
He was so good and so kind
He loved me like a husband
And a father, my only real love.

Mary L. Jackson

ODE TO A CAT

Be thankful for being alive and kicking
Be thankful for this place here
Be thankful for William Shakespeare, he was quite a guy
Be thankful for "a horse, a horse, my kingdom for a horse!"
Be thankful that you're not a cat, though cats are very
   nice animals
See how he walks around here, how proud he is
He doesn't turn his tail around and run as dogs do

                     Eric Carlson

THE POETRY PLATFORM

If I were the President,
The first thing I would do,
I would have a prayer
And ask God to clean my heart
Before all the world and all the people
So the people could watch me
And see all the good things I'm doing.

If I were the President of the United States,
The first thing on the agenda
Is to try not to have bigotry
Among my fellow men.

If I were the President,
I would improve the condition of old people:
A lot could be done which wouldn't cost a fortune,
But it would need a great deal of thought.

If I were President,
I would make a meeting with all the people
To see what the style of today is—
And everyone would be happy,
And I would go lucky.

If I were President,
The first thing I would do is
I would control the pay of all elected officials
And not let the public go on strike
When you can give yourself a raise
And not go on strike.

If I were President,
I'd want to find out what the people want me to do.

If I were President,
The first thing I would do
Is create a council for all the young people
(No one listens to young people any more
Which is why they turn into juvenile delinquents)
I'd give them a place in Washington, D.C.,
And listen to them,
Get together and talk things over,
Give them a say-so and then
Straighten things out,
And there wouldn't be any more rebellions
The way there are now
Between black and white, and young and old.

If I were President—
I don't want to be President,
I don't want to tell people what to do.

If I were President,
I would try to right what's wrong.

I wish I could find one person
In this world
To heal my leg
For I fear that I am losing it
And this is no joke
And not politics either.

> Mary L. Jackson, William Ross,
> Elsie Dikeman, Yetta Schmier,
> Harry Siegel, Carmela Pagluca,
> Selena Griffith, Mary Tkalec, and
> Sammie French

THE WEATHER

I am the rain, and I come down,
And I make everything in the farm grow.
The rain is welcome to the flowers,
They can't live without it.
We wait for the rain to settle the dust.

Oh it's raining, let's run under shelter
And get our buckets out to catch the rainwater!
Cloud feels empty,
Earth is so dry it needs a drink.

And the sky is beautiful,
You sit there and watch the sun come out
And the boats coming in,
And it rains all the time in Niagara Falls.

> by the class

POEM

It feels good to make love when it rains.

Sam Rainey

I LOVE RAIN

Sometimes the rain reminds me of hail
I'm seeing hail the size of raindrops
And bird eggs.
The rain is like cut glass in the sun.
I love the rain because I love diamonds.

Leroy Burton

POEM

I love the rain
I was a farm girl
always on the field.
You always got a shower
it washed you down.
I love the feel of it
and how clean it smells afterward.
We never had a bathtub,
we had a brook.
The bathing was beautiful—
men at night,
women by day.
We also had a deep swimming hole—
I swam like a fish.

Mary Tkalec

RAIN

Rain makes flowers' beauty open up
where I live in the country.
The rain hits the tin on the roof
we go to sleep listening to it.
Clouds clean everything out
when they rain.
Rain sounds like someone playing the organ:
all those mellow tones.

George Johnson

SLEEPING IN THE RAIN

It's so good to sleep when it rains
When the rain's coming down
Down on the houses
It's so beautiful to look out the window.

The house feels like a rocking chair
Going from side to side.

It feels so good when it rains
As long as you're inside.
After the rain, the green feels soft
And beautiful.
Rain is good for everything.

Sam Rainey

WEATHER

It washes the floors off.
Then when it gets dry

You can sit in the park when the benches get dry
And you can walk on the street when it stops.

It's like a person who goes to do everything—
That's how the sky is.
The sky gets busy, she's working,
She's raining.
Then, when it stops raining, she doesn't do anything.
The sky is the sky,
And the sun comes out again.

Yetta Schmier

WESTERN RAIN

When I lived on the West Coast
It rained for three solid months
All the way from Vancouver
Down to San Francisco.
In England it rains nearly all the time,
And in Niagara Falls the mist is like the rain.
I don't like rain all the time,
But it's necessary, like war,
Like cannons when they rain.

Eric Carlson

STORM

If I was the earth when it rains
I'd cry for rain
Because it makes all my flowers open up.
If I was the earth I wouldn't like storms
Because storms are cruel
To my neighbor flowers and my friends, the insects.

Sometimes they kill unnecessarily,
They drown things,
Whereas a sprinkle or shower is beautiful,
Just enough to drink.
Flowers are like human beings,
They need just enough water
To spring into beauty.

After a shower you see butterflies,
Ladybugs, all beautiful little insects,
And after a shower
All the crickets go in hiding until dark.
Then they come out with their music,
They go into a symphony,
They stretch and crawl and exercise their bodies,
They feel so refreshed after beautiful spring rain.

But in a storm all my earthly neighbors go into hiding
Under rocks and trees
Anywhere, for shelter.
They feel miserable
Unlike a shower, where they lie in the cool grass
And are refreshed and enjoy themselves,
Especially the crickets—
They get together and talk about the storm,
"Isn't this nasty weather we're having?"
"Yeah, sure is a shame we can't enjoy
The flowers and grass and all things that surround us.
Storm makes it too hard for us to walk,
That's why all of us insects love spring rain the best
And not storms, which are awful to everyone,
To all crawling things, to babies, men, and children,
And all human beings."

William Ross

POEM (to *Rhapsody in Blue*)

I like sitting here with my friend Harry.
I think it's always good to have good neighbors and
    friends—you included, of course.
You hear that music? Diddle-dee, diddle-dee,
Sounds so good.
There's so much you could say about music.
I could sit here all day and listen to it.

It makes me see happy people
Having a good time
Gathered in crowds
And again I could see
A storm coming up
And their parents calling out,
Come on, children, come on in.

Looks like Harry is dozing now.

It makes me think of all the young people out in parks
    and amusement places
And in the evening, going to each other's homes
And to ice-cream parlors, having ice-cream sodas,
Having a good time at the beaches.

I see myself sitting in a nice easy chair
Reading a book
And watching the people on the beaches, at the seashore
And dozing in-between:
Having a good time:
Something I can't do now, but will in the near future,
When I can see again.
And that's a day we're going to celebrate,

And Harry won't be able to take a nap—
We'll get him to do a jig for us!

Peggy Marriott

DREAMS

Sitting here listening to *Rhapsody in Blue*
by George Gershwin
reminds me of stormy weather,
of a rough rainstorm,
one where I couldn't go out and play.
We'd sit around the fireplace
listening to music
while Misty, our little angora kitten,
runs up and down the keyboard of our piano.
She looks like a ball of cotton.

The piano reminds me of rolling thunder,
the brass: the flashes of lightning.

This music makes me
remember my mother humming
an old folk song to me
while I'm in her arms.
The music was so sweet and smooth
that I fell asleep before she finished the song.
Listening to this music I can
imagine what the ending
of my mother's tune was
(when I fell asleep).

Now I am reminded of
the first ballet I ever saw,
Beauty and the Beast.
I can see the people on the stage,
all well-statured, beautiful to look at.
At first the ballet didn't appeal to me.
Now it's poetry in motion.
I wish I could see more ballet.
Rhapsody makes me think
of people all singing at once—
of joy, love, and dreams.

William Ross

DUET

My father once had a cat named Moose,
A big TOMCAT,
And he could whistle for him
Just like you whistle for a dog.
And my father would get a chair and sit down,
And when he came in, Moose would get in his lap.
Moose would whine, and my father would say:
Moose, where have you been,
I haven't seen you all day!
And they had the conversation on the front porch,
And nobody knew what they were talking about.

Fred Richardson

DELAPHINE, MY DAUGHTER

She used to say, I'm going to school today, Mamma
To get some education
So I won't sit around like you dummies.
I had seven children, but they all died.
Delaphine died at six from diphtheria.
If it had been today, they would have cured it,
And I would have had all those nice kids
To keep me company.

Mary L. Jackson

Poems from the
Lutheran Old Age Home
in Cedar Falls, Iowa

The people in the class at the Lutheran Old Age Home where I worked for one afternoon with the assistance of poet Anne Day were mostly in their seventies and eighties. Many were of Danish extraction, and some had been born in Denmark. All but a few were women. Most seemed in fairly good health. Some dictated their work and about half wrote their own. The I Never Told Anybody poem was a collaboration of the kind we had about Childhood Memories and Beautiful Things in the first class at the American Nursing Home. Everyone composed separately, without seeing other people's lines. Some, in writing their contributions, divided what they wrote into short lines, and these line divisions I've indicated by a slash (/). The poetry idea for the other poems, specific memories from different years of people's lives, is described at the end of the class on poems about growing older.

I NEVER TOLD ANYBODY

I told a friend I preferred going to a movie with a boy I loved instead of a legitimate show with another who wanted me.

The golden hue of a canary/and its sweet song at evening/ I never told anybody how much that canary meant to me—sweet, soft, it would lift my spirits.

I never told anyone that I was deeply hurt that my parents didn't believe in Santa Claus.

I never told anyone that I bluff my way through life.

I never told anyone that I can pray and my prayer will be answered like a miracle.

I never told anybody that when I was in Emporia, Kansas, I did meet somebody there when I went to college and for a good eight years we were very good friends, and we split. But now we write again. Don't tell anybody.

I might never have told anybody that I met Rainer, my husband to be, on board the ship, and when coming to Ellis Island someone took my arm and told me where to sit and someone took his arm and sat him right beside me. I took that as a good omen.

I never told anybody that I always looked up to my sister— I had other sisters, but she was the one. I know she felt that way about me—Petra.

I never told my mother she was beautiful. But to me she was the most beautiful in the world—She was in love with my father, who was a very handsome dark curly hair and blue eyes Scotch Irish by nature born in Yorktown . . .

I together with three of my friends was playing near a stream of water. We were all about eleven years old. One boy was jealous because two of us were probably too chummy. He started picking on me and continued until I became completely teed off. I grabbed his hat and very gently set it down on the water in the stream. He screamed out, "Oh that is my new hat." (He did get it out but I never learned how it looked after it dried.)

I never told anybody anything.

I spent hours on the radio/helping cooks I hope/how the cakes and pies were made!/and the thing that I have never told/is I was scared to death.

I never had an original idea in my life.

Carry me back to the harvest field/When the barn burned down, the heat from the fire stopped the chickens from laying and broke the glass thermometer by the porch door.

I never told anybody that I disliked poetry—I never cared to write it, really.

                                        by the class

When I was nineteen I lived in timber country in Northern Wisconsin in a log house ten miles out from town. Two of my four boys were born there.
I picked wild strawberries and sometimes a roast of deer meat was hung on the clothesline by a neighbor—in the dead of the night.
By the time I was forty we lived in town—David, Iowa—a very small town. I could see country from my window.
At sixty—there were grandchildren, but no more wild strawberries.

                                        Addie Reed

When I was ten years old
I looked at the huge waves of the ocean

They frightened me as I looked at it
Day after day.

When I was twenty years old
I came home and found trees lying all over the street
   where I lived
But we were all safe and sound.
The tornado was over.

                    Marie Mortensen

AS I GROW OLDER

When I was ten I had a small black dog.
When I was twenty-two I fell in love.
When I am eighty-seven I am content.

                    Fay Magee

When I was forty I had a dresser my parents had when they
   were married.
When I was eighty-eight I had a special chest of drawers
   made from an oak bedstead of my parents.

                    Elise Tange

When I was forty
I quit having birthdays.
When I was ten years old
May was my favorite month
That was when I took off my winter underwear.

                    Clare Berg

I MADE THE GRADE

When I was ten I was so sure I would never measure up.
When I was twenty-one I was scared to death of life.
When I was seventy I felt life to be a breeze.

Agneta Jensen

When I was five, I had my first doll, but alas, it didn't last
  very long. My sister played with it and that was the
  end. When I was ten, I dreamed of dolls, with buggy
  and all.

When I was twenty I still dreamed of dolls, but now they
  were live dolls.
When I was thirty, my dream came true. I then had four.
And now they have multiplied to sixteen.

Henrietta Hansen

WE HAD NO CHOICE

When I was eight we never got a new hat—we always had
  to wear hand-me-down hats.
When I was twenty-five by that time I always picked out
  hats that had plumes. I always picked them, whether
  I liked them or not, they had to have a plume on them.
When I was fifty we got into the smaller hats, but I still
  liked to have feathers or plumes on them, if it could
  be arranged. Otherwise, I'd look for one with fur.

Alene Voss

My folks would never let me go to a movie, so I sneaked—
    I'd say I was twelve.
The first doll I had, my sister gave me when I was thirteen
    —it had real hair.
I was my own boss at twenty—I think I was.
At sixty-seven it's shaping up okay.

Ida Peterson

MY LIFE

I didn't like to keep house, so at sixteen I taught country
    school because I like children.
I think my teaching certificate was dated 1909.
My mother said, "Now you are going out into the world.
    Just keep the men's hands off of you.
If you always act as good as you look nothing will harm
    you."
I always wanted a red dress but Dad said no. Only bad
    girls wear red.
The first money I earned I bought some red material and
    made myself a red dress— and a pair of red shoes.
I had a rival. She had money, I didn't. But I knew I could
    play the organ better than she could, without any
    lessons. Just the old Fullerton's songbook at school.

Myrtle Conner Christiansen

The Poets

LAURA BRADSHAW has been in the nursing home since 1971.

LEROY BURTON, sixty-two, was born in Boston. He was a tailor and presser. He is blind and walks with a cane. He has been in the nursing home a year and a half.

ERIC CARLSON, eighty-three, was born in Stockholm, and came to America in 1910, when he was eighteen. He worked for a fur company, showing furs to buyers. Confined to a wheelchair, he has been in the nursing home for five years.

NADYA CATALFANO was born in Oxen Hills, Maryland. She is ninety-four years old. She lived in Panama for a while. She worked in her aunt's laundry. She is in a wheelchair and has been at the nursing home for three years.

ELSIE DIKEMAN, eighty-three, is from New York City. She always did office work till a year and a half ago, when she suffered a series of strokes. She has been in the nursing home about a year.

FANNIE FELDSTEIN, ninety, was born in Russia. She had a candy store in Greenwich Village.

SELENA GRIFFITH, ninety, was born in Barbados and has been in the nursing home for three years.

MARY L. JACKSON, ninety-three, was born in Macon, Georgia. Her mother died in childbirth, and she was brought up by her grandmother. She used to sew for a factory. She is in a wheelchair and has one arm in a sling.

GEORGE JOHNSON, sixty-five, was born in Georgia. He worked on the New York docks as a stevedore. He has been in the nursing home for about a year.

CARL KOCH, seventy-six, was born in Hamburg, Germany. He was a chef. He has been in the nursing home three years.

HELEN LESSER, seventy-three, was born in Philadelphia. She was a professional actress and lived in the East Sixties in New York. She has been in the nursing home for five years.

ROSE MACMILLAN, sixty-three, is from Glasgow, Scotland. She came to this country as a young girl, worked as a waitress and did domestic work. She is in a wheelchair and has been in the nursing home for about a year.

PEGGY MARRIOTT, seventy-two, was born in New Rochelle, New York. She was a housewife till she came to the nursing home about two years ago. Peggy's eyesight is bad and she uses a metal walker.

TOM O'NEIL, eighty-one, is from Philadelphia. He worked in a textile mill. He has been in the nursing home for a year.

CARMELA PAGLUCA, seventy-five, was born in New York City. She was a New York City schoolteacher. She has been in the nursing home less than a year.

SAM RAINEY, sixty-two, is from Chester, South Carolina. He was a cook whose specialty was roasting. He is in a wheelchair and has been in the nursing home five years.

FRED RICHARDSON, seventy-nine, was born in St. Augustine, Florida. He was a messenger. He has limited sight. He is in a wheelchair and has been in the nursing home for two years.

WILLIAM ROSS, fifty-nine, is from Norfolk, Virginia. He was a utility and maintenance man. He is in a wheelchair and has been at the nursing home for five years.

YETTA SCHMIER, seventy-four, was born in New York City. She was a seamstress for a milliner's shop. She has been in the nursing home for four years.

HARRY SIEGEL, seventy, was born and brought up on a farm in Stepney, Connecticut. He was a repairman. He has been in the nursing home three and a half years.

MIRIAM SULLIVAN, ninety-one, was born in Barbados, West Indies. She was a housewife. She has been in the nursing home for a year.

MARY TKALEC, eighty-nine, was born in Hungary. She has worked as a seamstress and as a cook. She also made scapulars for the church.

FLORENCE WAGNER, seventy-six, is from Rye, New York. She did office work at the Metropolitan Life Insurance Company, was married for thirty-four years, belonged to the Republican Club.

GEORGE WARGO, seventy-five, was born in Philipsburg, Pennsylvania. He worked in import-export and was a promoter. He is in a wheelchair and has been in the nursing home for a year and a half.

MARGARET WHITTAKER, fifty, was born in New York City. She was editorial assistant for a newspaper. She is confined to her wheelchair and has been at the nursing home for two years.

MARY ZAHORJKO, ninety-four, was born in Poland. She has been at the nursing home for two years.

Since these biographical notes were written, Tom O'Neil has died. Other students have died, whose poems, for one reason or another, we have not been able to include here: Fannie Goldstein, Kitty Hoblitzell, Minnie Malament and Marie Schaefer. And now, just as this book is about to be published, I have learned of the death of William Ross.

About the Author

KENNETH KOCH's books of poetry include *The Pleasures of Peace, Thank You and Other Poems, Ko, or A Season on Earth, The Art of Love,* and, most recently, *The Duplications.* He is also the author of a book of plays, *A Change of Hearts;* a novel, *The Red Robins;* and two outstanding books on education, *Wishes, Lies, and Dreams: Teaching Children to Write Poetry* and *Rose, Where Did You Get That Red? Teaching Great Poetry to Children.* He lives in New York City and is a Professor of English at Columbia University.

VINTAGE BIOGRAPHY AND AUTOBIOGRAPHY

V-2024 **CARO, ROBERT A.** / The Power Broker: Robert Moses and the Fall of New York

V-608 **CARR, JOHN DICKSON** / The Life of Sir Arthur Conan Doyle

V-888 **CLARKE, JOHN HENRIK (ed.)** / Marcus Garvey and the Vision of Africa

V-261 **COHEN, STEPHEN F.** / Bukharin and the Bolshevik Revolution: A Political Biography

V-746 **DEUTSCHER, ISAAC** / The Prophet Armed

V-748 **DEUTSCHER, ISAAC** / The Prophet Outcast

V-617 **DEVLIN, BERNADETTE** / The Price of My Soul

V-2023 **FEST, JOACHIM C.** / Hitler

V-225 **FISCHER, LOUIS (ed.)** / The Essential Gandhi

V-132 **FREUD, SIGMUND** / Leonardo Da Vinci

V-969 **GENDZIER, IRENE L.** / Franz Fanon

V-979 **HERZEN, ALEXANDER** / My Past and Thoughts (Abridged by Dwight Mac-donald)

V-268 **JUNG, C. G.** / Memories, Dreams, Reflections

V-728 **KLYUCHEVSKY, V.** / Peter the Great

V-280 **LEWIS, OSCAR** / Children of Sanchez

V-634 **LEWIS, OSCAR** / A Death in the Sanchez Family

V-92 **MATTINGLY, GARRETT** / Catherine of Aragon

V-151 **MOFFAT, MARY JANE AND CHARLOTTE PAINTER (eds.)** / Revelations: Diaries of Women

V-151 **PAINTER, CHARLOTTE AND MARY JANE MOFFAT (eds.)** / Revelations: Diaries of Women

V-677 **RODINSON, MAXINE** / Mohammed

V-847 **SNOW, EDGAR** / Journey to the Beginning

V-411 **SPENCE, JONATHAN** / Emperor of China: Self-Portrait of K'ang-hsi

V-133 **STEIN, GERTRUDE** / The Autobiography of Alice B. Toklas

V-826 **STEIN, GERTRUDE** / Everybody's Autobiography

V-100 **SULLIVAN, J. W. N.** / Beethoven: His Spiritual Development

V-287 **TAYLOR, A. J. P.** / Bismarck: The Man and the Statesman

V-275 **TOKLAS, ALICE B. AND EDWARD BURNS (ed.)** / Staying on Alone: Letters of Alice B. Toklas

V-951 **WATTS, ALAN** / In My Own Way: An Autobiography

V-327 **WINSTON, RICHARD AND CLARA** / Letters of Thomas Mann 1899-1955

VINTAGE CRITICISM: LITERATURE, MUSIC, AND ART

V-570   **ANDREWS, WAYNE** / American Gothic
V-418   **AUDEN, W. H.** / The Dyer's Hand
V-887   **AUDEN, W. H.** / Forewords and Afterwords
V-161   **BROWN, NORMAN O.** / Closing Time
V-75   **CAMUS, ALBERT** / The Myth of Sisyphus and Other Essays
V-626   **CAMUS, ALBERT** / Lyrical and Critical Essays
V-535   **EISEN, JONATHAN** / The Age of Rock: Sounds of the American Cultural Revolution
V-4   **EINSTEIN, ALFRED** / A Short History of Music
V-13   **GILBERT, STUART** / James Joyce's Ulysses
V-407   **HARDWICK, ELIZABETH** / Seduction and Betrayal: Women and Literature
V-114   **HAUSER, ARNOLD** / Social History of Art, Vol. I
V-115   **HAUSER, ARNOLD** / Social History of Art, Vol. II
V-116   **HAUSER, ARNOLD** / Social History of Art, Vol. III
V-117   **HAUSER, ARNOLD** / Social History of Art, Vol. IV
V-610   **HSU, KAI-YU** / The Chinese Literary Scene
V-201   **HUGHES, H. STUART** / Consciousness and Society
V-88   **KERMAN, JOSEPH** / Opera as Drama
V-995   **KOTT, JAN** / The Eating of the Gods: An Interpretation of Greek Tragedy
V-685   **LESSING, DORIS** / A Small Personal Voice: Essays, Reviews, Interviews
V-677   **LESTER, JULIUS** / The Seventh Son, Vol. I
V-678   **LESTER, JULIUS** / The Seventh Son, Vol. II
V-720   **MIRSKY, D. S.** / A History of Russian Literature
V-118   **NEWMAN, ERNEST** / Great Operas, Vol. I
V-119   **NEWMAN, ERNEST** / Great Operas, Vol. II
V-976   **QUASHA, GEORGE AND JEROME ROTHENBERG (eds.)** / America A Prophecy: A New Reading of American Poetry from Pre-Columbian Times to the Present
V-976   **ROTHENBERG, JEROME AND GEORGE QUASHA (eds.)** / America A Prophecy: A New Reading of American Poetry from Pre-Columbian Times to the Present
V-415   **SHATTUCK, ROGER** / The Banquet Years, Revised
V-435   **SPENDER, STEPHEN** / Love-Hate Relations: English and American Sensibilities
V-278   **STEVENS, WALLACE** / The Necessary Angel
V-100   **SULLIVAN, J. W. N.** / Beethoven: His Spiritual Development
V-166   **SZE, MAI-MAI** / The Way of Chinese Painting
V-162   **TILLYARD, E. M. W.** / The Elizabethan World Picture